IT'S ALL ABOUT THE CHILDREN

Margaret B. Hill

EPIPHANY PUBLISHING HOUSE

Write the author
Margaret Hill
P.O. Box 726
Patton, California 92369

Epiphany Publishing House
P.O. Box 2383
Rancho Cucamonga, California 91729

ISBN 978-0-578-08532-6
Library of Congress Control Number:

1st Printing 2011
Printed in the U.S.A.

~ *My Supporters* ~

I hope you find my first publication a joy and easy reading. I made every attempt to provide a book that would not require a lot of you time. Your support will make it possible for students to benefit from the profits. Fifty percent of the profit will be given equally to a scholarship fund, which will probably be the Margaret B. Hill Scholarship Fund and Maggie's Kids Foundation.

Maggie's Kids Foundation is already a 501 (c) 3 nonprofit organization and has been in existence since 2003. Criteria for a scholarship fund have to be implemented.

Write the author

Margaret Hill

P.O. Box 726

Patton, California 92369

~ *Dedication* ~

This book is dedicated in memory of my mother and father, Roosevelt and Sophia Willis Bynum. Even though we were sharecroppers, they made sure that we never knew we were poor. Well actually, I guess we weren't since we had as much as the next sharecropper.

As an adult, I seek to adopt a quote from someone famous that would guide how I live my life. "We must struggle to begin our lives in less selfish and more purposeful ways, redefining success by national and individual character and service rather than by national consumption and the superficial barriers of race and class."

The Measure of Our Success

By Marian Wright Edelman

~Acknowledgements ~

How can I ever say "thank you" enough to the people, past and present, who have had such a profound effect on my life's journey?

To my wonderful, loving family, I owe you such an enormous debt of gratitude for all of the joy and laughter and memorable times we have enjoyed together.

To my late parents who were responsible for my birth and made sure I went to college because they never thought I would find a husband. I know they would have been very proud, but not at all shocked by my accomplishments and of the many young lives I have touched along the way. They might have been surprised that I did find a good man.

To my husband, Robert Hill, thank you for the good times we shared over the years and for all of the encouragement and support I received from you while writing this book.

Thanks to my sisters, Viola and Clasteen, who financially supported me while I was in college because they so wanted me to succeed, to do great things for myself and others, and to enjoy fun things in my life.

Thank you Buddy for always sending me $100 every Christmas because I took care of your son from the time he was two days old until he was almost 10 years old.

Thanks to my brother, Linwood (Adell), for supporting and encouraging my ambitions to help children from all walks of life and for getting my Tiger Woods autograph.

Thanks to my cousin, Randolph Peete, who gave me a wealth of information about the Bynum family.

Thanks to my brother Raymond (ValJean), who let me know that being the youngest child wasn't all that bad.

I have written about many students who identified with the names of my nieces and nephews: Ricky (deceased), Larry, Monica, Veronica, Kenneth, Erika, Diana (deceased), Raymond, Eddie, Christina, Anthony, Craig, Gregory, Karen (deceased), Darren, Sandra, Hezekiah, and Aaron. The grand nieces and nephews I know and some I don't know, are: Andrew, Robert, Monique, Tamika, Chantelle, Marlo, Patrick, Bryan, Vanessa, Al, Jasmine, Breanna, Ben, Edwin, Cheryl Lynn, Ca'sha, Courtney, Edward, Keiasha, Darnell, Julia, and Sonja.

My book should make the best seller's list after my relatives purchase one for themselves and at least two for their friends. It is within the context of this book that I begin today reliving my life. To all who have inspired me to be the very best I can, I give thanks.

~ Forward ~

Brenda Gray, a former teacher at San Andreas High School and now works for the State of New Mexico asked permission to write the forward. She and all the teachers, classified staff and counselors had a profound impact on my life. Even though we did not all share the same philosophy, we knew our mission was to make life better for all the young people we came in contact with.

I first met Margaret Hill in the fall of 2000. My youngest daughter was attending a university in a nearby township close to San Bernardino. She was not having the best of times. I was living in a Best Western Hotel until she decided if she was going to stay or go. My daughter was a young black tennis player in the land of money and class. I was blessed to land a job with the San Bernardino School District, but placed in a school I wasn't strong enough to cope with. The kids were great. I left knowing there were a few I had touched.

I loved the administrators and the staff at the Central Office from the superintendent on down. They had all gone over and beyond to accommodate my requests; approve advances when I got in financial dire straights. The day I was granted a transfer to San Andreas High School was the day I no longer had to fend my battles, and those of my daughters alone. Margaret Hill, and often times her husband, Bob, were always there.

She became my friend, my confidante, and my mentor. "Maggie", as we grew to call her, taught me a whole lot about patience, diplomacy, and real love for children. As a whole, San Andreas had a competent and caring staff, but there was often times too much unnecessary drama. A lot of the times, I was in the center of it all, not by choice I must add. Some of the greatest kids I have ever been involved with I met at San Andreas. Kids who lived in group homes; gang members; young mothers and fathers; kids who read at a 3rd and 4th grade level; but kids who were so beautiful inside and continued to hold on to hope and any sign of "I care" they could get.

Before a student could get into San Andreas, a parent or guardian and the student had to meet Maggie first. Sometimes she went against popular opinion or the grain to let a kid in. No matter where she goes in the area and including Las Vegas, there is always someone who will know Margaret Hill and remember all of the great things she achieved.

What I have always admired about her is that she seemed to simplify life in such an organized way. Each day seemed always filled, and most of the time involved a child. Many children have been touched in some way by this "guru" in the field of education and "real love" for children. Quite a few lives have been turned around because this wonderful silver haired lady who has been known to slam a kid against the fence rather than to see him expelled for fighting and then continuing the fight off school grounds, cared about them more than they cared about themselves. Difference would be resolved or they both would stay in a locked office until parents or guardians arrived.

There were teachers and staff members Maggie held onto and overlooked because she recognized they did good things with the kids and the kids were the ones that mattered. No doubt, she had naysayers, especially after "Maggie's Café" opened, and "Maggie's Kids Foundation" was formed. As I said, for Mrs. Hill, "it's all about the children".

The language in this book

are not grammatical errors, but conversational slang….

~ Chapter One ~

The world is round and the place which may seem like the end

may also be only the beginning - Ivy Baker Priest

It started quite sometime ago in the State of Virginia. I was the fifth child born, and based on past history of the family, I should've been the last.

Linwood was the first born; Viola came two years, three months later. Then Kenneth (Buddy) was born fifteen months later; Clasteen was born 19 months later; and 15 months later, I entered the world. Linwood vividly remembers the day I was born. He said Uncle Randall drove his mule and cart, his only means of transportation, to Newsome, the nearest town to get the doctor to assist the midwife with my delivery. I was told that my dad was working as a cook and the gardener at school that day. My brother recalls the mule being beaten and running extremely fast to get this tiny, old country doctor back to the house.

Since it had been nearly two years since a baby had been born in the Bynum home, it was determined that I would definitely be the last. Hence, I was tagged with the nickname "Babysis". I later found out that my oldest brother gave me that name because he couldn't say "Margaret." Six years later, this chubby person who did not look like any of the dolls we played with was suddenly in the house. I remember crying, and saying, "*He* cheated me out of being babysis", the name that I'd grown to love.

I vaguely remember my paternal grandmother and maternal grandfather, but after having the opportunity to travel on the Underground Railroad later in life, I was able to look up my ancestors in the Hamilton County Library Archives, I became even more curious about my family history. My father's eighty-six year old cousin also provided me with a great deal of information. My great-grandmother, Ida Murray, lived to be a grand old age of 110; my father's mother, Martha, died when she was 75. My grandfather, Randall, only lived sixty or so years. They were all reared in Murfreesboro and Princeton, North Carolina.

To my knowledge, Charlie Peete, my cousin, and brother to Randolph was the only famous member of our family. Sadly, his fame was short-lived. Charlie was a professional baseball player for the St. Louis Cardinals. No one knew exactly what happened, or why he was so insistent that his family accompany him to Venezuela where he was to train, but the airplane crashed, killing the entire family. My memory will never erase those five white caskets inside the church, and people filing in for the funeral services. Charlie Peete and his family would always remain in our hearts.

I also discovered I had seven great aunts: Henrietta, Laura, Annie, Dora, Lucy, Molly, and Martha. My dad had three sisters: Henrietta, Annie Mae, and Esther, and three brothers: James, Randall, and Glynnis. I had only one great uncle, Louis Murray, on my dad's side.

I was pleased to acquire some information about my mom's side of the family from my cousin, John Lee. They lived in Handsome, Virginia, and were part of the Bryant Plantation. My mother had one sister, who died at the age of eighteen, and four brothers: John, Leroy, Willie, and Pompy. One of my relatives was very light skinned with naturally curly hair. He lived in Mt. Vernon, New York and would visit us once a year. We often wondered how he got in the family with those features, so when my cousin told me about the Bryant Plantation, I understood.

One of his sons, Kenneth, always visited us during the summer. One summer, my brother, Buddy (Kenneth), was standing on the back porch with the rest of us when my city cousin, Kenneth, decided to show us how a hangman's noose worked. My brother kicked the chair away, causing my cousin to dangle. He probably would have died had it not been for my mother. She came just in time to put the chair down below his feet. This incident reminded me of one of my former students who had been having difficulty getting his life together. His mother called me to say he would not be in school due to an illness. When I questioned just how ill he was, his mother informed me that John had attempted suicide. When he returned to school some time later, he unashamedly showed me the rope burns on his neck.

I was raised on a farm during my early childhood and school days, and for the first few years of my life, we lived without electricity and indoor toilets. When we finally did get electricity, it took only one year for the faulty wiring to start a fire. We lost everything except my little brother's guitar and the electric stove my dad had won at a new department store grand opening. When the fire broke out, all of my siblings were at school except my oldest brother who was in the Army and my oldest sister who was working in New Jersey.

When I was extremely young and had not started school yet, I would listen for the farm bell to ring letting the farmers know it was time to check in for lunch. Most of the time, I knew that would be the time my dad would first find a switch (a dreadfully long and thin wooden item used for punishment for bad behavior), and then drive to the elementary school to question what one of my brothers had done to disrupt the educational process. He always seemed to be in trouble. Wherever I was, I would always run as fast as I could and wait for my dad by his car. After he took care of my brother, he would return to the farm where he continued with his duties as a sharecropper, and I continued to play in the yard by myself. This all happened prior to my fifth year in the world since I would attend school after that.

Looking back at the days of those whippings, or corporal punishment as we know it today, it reminds me of my first assignment at the middle school where I was vice principal, and it was politically correct to punish a student by using the paddle. I only initiated this punishment to a few deserving students, but I remember fondly the last one who decided to have a friendly conversation with me as he leaned over and held the chair. I realized then that this punishment was ineffective and cruel. I should have known better because it never helped my brother either. What was fascinating was that in spite of my brother's terrible behavior and defiance, he was quite intelligent.

I attended a two-room schoolhouse from grades one through seven. We walked and shared stories on the way. One of the daily discussions I can remember was with the white students since all schools were segregated. They were waiting for the school bus as we took the long walk to school. We exchanged what was happening in the respective schools. We were always friendly and incredibly respectful of each other. We accepted the fact that schools were segregated institutions.

I began school at the age of five only because my father was the cook and the gardener for the school. My birthday came in December which meant I was suppose to start school the next school year. One teacher was in charge of grades one through three, and all the students were educated in one classroom. She was young and attractive, but I felt she just didn't like me, and it was probably because I was not an excellent student and somewhat lazy. If we didn't do our homework, we had to line up, hold out our hand and get our ten swats with the ruler. My sister had outstanding academic abilities, so she managed to laugh at me. When I got to the next teacher, who taught grades four through seven in the other classroom, things did not get much better. She was an older woman but was pleasant and seemed to like me more than my first teacher. I had difficulty learning and school was a challenge for me.

My sister, Clasteen, would not help me except when students would pick on me for whatever reason. She would approach me at the end of the school day and ask, "Who bothered you today?" I would give her the person's name and the fight was on. She and I fought a lot, but she always protected me at school. She was just one grade ahead of me, so when she went to high school, which began with the 8th grade, I spent one year running home daily to keep from getting in a fight, something I knew I would not successfully accomplish. In addition to not being the sharpest knife in the drawer, I couldn't even fight. I didn't realize I was such a coward until I became an adult. I had a soft spot for students who didn't want to fight, and I felt most of them did not. I can remember the student who waited while the other girl fixed her dress strap before they continued the fight. On another occasion, a student asked the girl she was to fight to give her time to put her glasses in the case, so they would not get broken. I also remember the student who invited students to her home to fight. They showed up, a whole car load. The girl was glad her father was home. There was another situation where a small, short, high school student would always challenge those students who were bigger, taller, and stronger. Andrew would fight on campus or in the neighborhood. One day I followed this group and suggested that he come with me. He refused. As usual, he got beaten again. I learned just recently that this is an indication of self-mutilation.

Some students managed to use their parents to fight their battles. That reminds me of the conference that I had with a student and his parent about his ability to do class work. Sam asked his mom to meet with me regarding his inability to be successful at the alternative high school. We talked about Sam's behavior and had come to what we considered were good solutions when Sam said, "Mom, go ahead and tell her."

"Tell her what?" Mom asked.

"You know, the math."

"Oh yeah, Mrs. Hill, Sam cannot do the math, and I know it is hereditary as I cannot do the math myself."

I said, "My mom quit school when she was in the seventh grade and my father quit when he was in the third grade. I still learned how to read, so I'm not buying that. I wasn't good in math either but it wasn't hereditary, it was laziness. Your son has the same disease, and it is curable."

When I finished elementary school, we had an opportunity to ride the bus to the high school that was about twenty miles away. I can remember socializing to and from school. It was a thrill thinking of the nice ride to high school but I soon discovered that the fun was gone because you had to sit down and be quiet on the bus. Even though, I understand the importance of integration, busing has destroyed one segment of the social system because young people cannot laugh, talk, play, joke, run and walk while on the bus. The rules regarding bus transportation have not changed; therefore, it was not unusual for me to intercept when necessary. The boys' basketball team failed to win the championship, and was returning to the school when they felt a need to use profanity, and not obey the rules of the bus driver nor the coach. The driver exited the freeway and called the city police. I received a call and agreed to meet the bus. The coach drove my car home while I rode on the bus and dared any student to say one word.

We attended a two-story brick high-school for grades eight through eleven at which time we were granted a high-school diploma. We were in school from 9 am until 3:30 daily. It was strange having a male teacher since I had not seen one the first seven years of school. The four teachers I remember the most were my music teacher, my science teacher, my shorthand teacher, and another teacher who was the only one who truly liked me, but I cannot remember what she taught. I assumed that she liked me because she often asked if she could take me home on the weekends. We didn't have hot running water, so it might have just been to clean me up. The music teacher gave us a senior assignment that was due the day before graduation and consisted of a one-thousand word report. Can you believe he counted every word and would not give us a grade until we had the expected count? My science teacher would write extremely small on the chalkboard, and we had to fill in the missing word. The shorthand teacher just thought I was dumb and not capable of mastering the subject. I received a failing grade the first reporting period, but I was so fascinated with shorthand, I taught myself. By the time I left high school, I had been taking dictation at one-hundred words a minute.

What I remembered the most was being in the shadow of my sister who was brilliant and had many skills including dancing, singing and playing basketball. She had the long hair and the beautiful white teeth while I had to wear braids/corn rows as my hair was short. I could not do any of those; however, during a school event, I represented the seniors at the school Olympics in the fifty-yard dash. I don't think anyone was surprised when I came in last place. I also remembered the day my brother received three days of after-school detention because he asked one of his teachers, "How long do you think it will be before man walks on the moon?" The teacher responded, "Three days of detention for asking such a dumb question." The thing that bothered me the most about school was the seating chart, which meant I was constantly in front of the classroom because my last name began with the letter "b". Being short didn't have any perks either as I was always in the front of the line when we had to line up for activities. I had very few friends in high school and cannot think of anything that happened there that I want repeated. I was ready to leave home and did not have plans of returning except to visit my family. I attended my first high school reunion twenty-five years later, and nothing had changed. There were one or two classmates who remembered me and the ones who were popular in high school still ran the show.

My mother insisted that I attend the nearest college, which was about sixty miles from where we lived. I said, "No way." My teachers, all of them, had done an excellent job of assuring me that I would not make it in college and that I should seek employment in one of the local factories. That reminded me of more instances where students who became successful was given the same advice that I was given. One was told she would never make it in law school; however, she passed the bar on her first attempt. Another was told he was not Harvard material; however, he graduated in three years, and with honors. Another student received his doctorate after his counselor laughed at him when he mentioned he wanted to attend University of California-Davis.

While I believed them, my mother did not, and suggested that I attend the college not far from home and earn a secretarial certificate so that I could get an office job. My mother knew I was a speedy typist and could do shorthand at about one hundred words a minute when I left high school. On the other hand, my teachers witnessed my poor grammar and average grades before making the assessment about what my career plans should be. My mother insisted and in those days, parents always won the battle.

While attending college, I participated in sit-in demonstrations. This was tremendously important to me for several reasons: we were treated as second-class citizens in more ways than one. We could not eat at any restaurant unless it was owned by someone of the same race. We could not drink from the same water fountains nor could we use the same restrooms. We couldn't even sit together at the movie theater. We had to sit upstairs while the whites were downstairs. The only place that was not segregated was the drive-in theaters. The public schools were closed down, and the department stores made it obvious that they did not want our business. We couldn't try on shoes, including summer sandals, unless our feet were covered. We could not try on hats at all. We had separate beaches and of course our own place on the back of the bus. While traveling to and from college from my small hometown, we had to wait in separate waiting rooms and use separate restroom facilities and restaurant.

I graduated from college in 1963 and attempted to get a job teaching.

Schools had become integrated in the Norfolk area and since I had a business education degree, and had considerable typing and shorthand skills, I felt I had a excellent chance of getting a job; however, schools were only obligated to hire a certain number of teachers of color. It was not surprising to me when one of my classmates at Old Dominion College in graduate school, suggested that I apply for a job where he was working, there was a need for teachers. After the principal asked my ethnicity, he told me that he had hired his quota, but thanks for calling. We do not always appreciate the truth, but we should always value the honesty of people.

I can remember one student who came to me with a sad look one morning.

"What's wrong?" I asked.

"I got stopped by the police last night. I wasn't doing anything wrong."

"I didn't think the police could stop and harassed you if you are not speeding or breaking the law. I am usually just a few blocks from my home and had not been speeding. I have a driver's license and my car is registered. Do you think they stop me because my car is old and maybe I had the music a little too loud?"

I responded, "Don't you think it is time to get a haircut so that the police will leave you alone? A lot of people are driving old cars. Besides, the music is loud in most cars driven by anyone under the age of twenty-five." I explained.

"There's nothing wrong with my hair. I have a right to wear dreadlocks."

"The police have the right to stop you. If you don't want to get a haircut, stop driving and have someone provide your transportation." I said.

I received a stare that inferred, "That's a dumb comment."

Two weeks later, the student had a nice clean haircut, and we both chuckled.

"Tired of the police, I see."

"Yes, Mrs. Hill, I'm going to see if you know what you are talking about."

This student never received a ticket nor was he stopped by police for the remainder of his school career.

I attempted to let all students know that life might not be fair, and no one ever said it would be, therefore, you should pick the battles you know you can win.

~ Chapter Two ~

I had a lucrative career in education and the private sector; however, beginning with my first job, I learned the importance of a good education. As the daughter of a sharecropper, we had numerous chores. I was designated as the one to baby-sit my younger brother, Raymond, who should not have existed.

My most memorable moment as a sitter was when we had a rooster that I did not like and was determined to put him in his place one day. My plan was to hit the rooster with the broom and then run into the house with my little brother. My parents and siblings had all gone to work in the fields picking cotton and the two of us were left alone. Well, part of the idea materialized when I threw the broom in hopes of frightening the rooster. When I missed and the rooster started chasing me, I became scared as we had no place to hide. Someone in the family had locked the front door of the house. My little brother and I sought refuge between the locked door and the screen door for a few hours until my family got close enough to hear both of us crying. Until then, the rooster just pecked away at items on the ground but never gave us enough space to escape.

This reminds me of the many times I asked students to make sure they had a workable plan before finalizing their decision. One student informed me that he was going to get a fake ID, a fake high school diploma and move to Canada to get his life together. He would then return to California and begin his life with new skills, a diploma that was accepted in Canada, and plenty of money to assist his family. What he failed to do was check on the background and lifestyle of his girlfriend who was in the automobile with him when he was murdered.

Years later, when I was a high-school principal, a student called me about 7:30 am. He was hiding from a car full of young men in their twenties who pulled up next to him at the bus stop and asked, "Where are you from?"

When the student responded that he was not in a gang, someone in the car pointed a gun at his head; however, he managed to jump the fence at an auto repair shop, cross the street and run into the grocery store. One of the office staff stated, "Mrs. Hill, you have a call from a student and it sounds like he is crying. Even though he was crying, I understood him to say, "Mrs. Hill, I'm scared. They are going to kill me." I said, "Stay in the store. I'll be there to get you."

I got in my sedan and without discussing my destination, I yelled. "I'll be right back." I traveled to where I asked the student to wait for me but did not see him. As I made my second u-turn, I saw John in a white car and was hesitant to approach it.

The driver of the car said, "Its okay. I'm his friend and we are waiting for you.

"Thanks." I responded.

John looked around and then got in my car. While transporting him to school and because he was so upset, I did not ask any questions about the incident. When we were within a few blocks of the school, John said, "Mrs. Hill, the car is behind us now."

"What are you talking about?"

"That's the car they were in".

"We will go to Patton State Hospital. They have police there."

As I prepared to make a left turn on Central, John said, "That's not them, but that car sure looks like the one."

We both let out a sigh of relief.

I transported John home after calling his mother. That experience was terribly frightening to me.

The rooster episode also reminds me of the time that I discovered a snake in the cafeteria. One student had a difficult time getting to class on his own.

Every morning after his mother walked him to the office; I would give him a few seconds and then follow him to class. This particular day he decided to leave campus by the cafeteria, and since I had seen him, I decided to go into the cafeteria and walk up behind him. As I was exiting the east door, I realized I was not alone and decided to look in the corner by the door. There was a large garden snake curled in the corner. I yelled to the student, "Come here! Come right now!"

He turned around and said, "I'm going to class now."

I said, "No, don't go to class, come here."

He was as afraid of the snake as I was. One of the teachers was told that a snake was in the cafeteria. He released the snake in the grassy area near the school.

My second job was working on the farm where we raised not only animals but corn, cotton, and peanuts. We all hated the work and did not look forward to holidays because we knew we would be working in the fields. The first few years of my life were lived without electricity and indoor toilets. The day finally came when we got electricity, and it took just one year for the faulty wiring to start a fire. We lost everything except my little brother's guitar and the electric stove my dad had won at a new department store grand opening. All of my siblings were at school except my oldest brother who was in the Army and my oldest sister who was working in New Jersey.

When the Old Fire occurred in San Bernardino County in 2003, we were evacuated, and that experience was just as devastating. I first saw the fire from the freeway as I was leaving a meeting. I saw how progressive the fire became so when I entered the house, I began packing pictures, birth certificates and other valuables that were not in the vault. I also stored two pillows and a few blankets in the car along with toiletries and changes of clothes for my husband and me. I then sat on the curb and watched the fire come closer to the house. It was not long after I notified my family by e-mail that I was sure we would have to evacuate that the word came. We spent the night in Moreno Valley. That fire reminded me of the middle school student who chose to leave campus and smoke a cigarette in the vacant field near the school. He started a fire then ran, leaving his evidence, his jacket. Another student threw a lit firecracker which landed in the rear of the classroom. Students refused to identify the student until I told them that same person will probably bring a firecracker again the next day and the aim may not be as great. In fact, it probably would land in someone's hair. Before I returned to my office, I had the name of the suspect.

My parents built a house in the next largest city which was still under 3,000 people and, yes, we did have electricity but did not have indoor toilets nor did we have hot and cold running water. We still had a water pump attached to our porch where we could get water.

Life was different in the big city of 3,000 people. I never knew I was poor until I moved there because there were the "haves" and the "have not's." It was a different culture altogether. I remember the first visit to my friend's home on a Sunday afternoon where they were having fried chicken for lunch. That was unheard of because you only ate fried foods for breakfast. The other two meals included baked or boiled meats. The grocery stores were enormous, and my parents had to spend at least $10 each time they went there. While on the farm, we made everything including our soap from the hog fat, and our clothes from the flour sacks bags. We only purchased flour, cheese and molasses. We did not have a cow, so we got our milk from one of the neighbors.

Since we no longer lived on the farm, we could work for others. I picked strawberries one day for about ten hours. For every strawberry, I put in the basket, I put two in my mouth so needless to say, when the day was over, I only made 95 cents. My next job was a paper route carrier where

I earned ten cents for every newspaper that I sold. They only sent me twenty papers so the most I could make was $2.00 and that was a weekly paper.

~ Chapter Three ~

I graduated from Hayden High School in Franklin, Virginia, at the age of sixteen and looked forward to moving away from home. It was decided by my mother that I would attend Norfolk State College in Norfolk, Virginia, and I would major in secretarial science and complete the program in two years. When we visited the school, we were provided the name of a family that was looking for someone to work for room and board. The college did not have dormitories at that time; however, some students were able to reside in the Young Women's Christian Association (YWCA) which was located across the street. I moved into the home of a family of four where the mother worked at the college, the father was a high-school coach, and the two students (boy and girl) attended the local public schools. My responsibilities were to clean house and do laundry when I was not in school. I did not have the time to participate in extracurricular activities, because I had to report to the house as soon as school was out. I could do my chores and still have time for homework. I was interested in becoming a member of the drill team; however, my "opportunity home" family did not think I should take time away from them to participate in this activity. I am usually not strong willed; however, being in the drill team was one of the things I wanted to do. They gave in and allowed me to participate.

The opportunity homeowners and I did not agree on having a dog in the house so when the dog had an accident one night, and when I went toschool the next day without cleaning up the mess, I was in trouble. It did not help when I was asked, "What should you do when you get up in the morning, and there is dog waste on the floor?" I responded, "It would not happen to me because I would never keep a dog in the house." When I wenthome for Christmas break, the news came that I would need to find anotherplace to live. I spent the second semester in a home that was owned by a minister who lived in one of the rooms, rented the downstairs to a Navy family and the remainder of the upstairs to three of us girls. I stayed there for the rest of the school year, and then moved in with the family of a good friend.

I located my next job by perusing the phone book looking for a job as a shampoo girl in a beauty parlor. That was the only skill I had at that time. You see, my sister, and I would take care of each other's hair. I found two wonderful women who gave me an opportunity to work Friday after school and all day Saturday. When school started for my second year of college, I was without a place to stay, and my mother suggested that I move in with a cousin, my mother's cousin, a much older woman. She was part Indian but somewhat eccentric I thought. When my friends came to see me, if she answered the doorbell, she began teaching them.

"I came by to see Margaret."

"Don't you think that you should ask me how am I doing?"

"Sure, Is Margaret in?"

"Who are your parents? I will only allow people with influential parents to enter my home."

"Tell Margaret that I will see her at school tomorrow."

"The door slams."

Needless to say, my visiting friends came to a halt. One Saturday while working my job at the beauty salon, I shared my poor relationship with my cousin. I told the operators that I was miserable there and that I was not allowed to have friends. I shared that my cousin was crazy, and we all laughed. When I showed up at breakfast the next morning, my cousin, and I had the strangest conversation.

"How are you this morning? My cousin asked."

"I'm fine. What about you?"

"Well, even though I am crazy, I still fixed your breakfast."

"I have a lot of studying to do today", I said.

"Even though I am crazy, I'll make sure that you're not disturbed."

I thought, "What a weird conversation."

"Why would you allow the people you worked with talk about me?"

"What are you talking about? I asked."

"When you talk about people in a beauty salon, you need to know who's in there."

"I know I said things that I should not have said, but who do you know that heard me?"

"Look out the window."

I saw the neighbor that I did not know, and she had delivered my message. I had to pack again, and this time I rented a room from a stranger.

I also worked part-time as a car hop at the local drive-in restaurant. I had to pay my own rent because my mother was frustrated with me for not being able to maintain living quarters. It was at the beauty salon, that I met a lady who told me that she knew someone in real estate, who was in need of an office clerk. I worked in this real estate office part-time until I graduated from high school. During the summer months, I would go to New York and work cleaning homes and babysitting.

I graduated from college in 1963 and immediately went to work for a local bank. That's where I was when John F. Kennedy was assassinated, also when the leader of the Dominican Republic was killed.

That job as a bank teller was interesting and frustrating. I was the first Black teller, and I just don't think people trusted me with their money. For my first few months, I always felt like a monkey in the cage as the lines in the bank would be long, and no one wanted to come to my window. One by one, people began to trust me and, as you may know, my line became the long one in the bank. The skills I learned there were helpful when I began working for the school district. I already knew how to be patient with staff, students, and parents. I felt I was never at a loss for words, and did not have a problem apologizing.

I can remember the parent who got upset at me for telling her daughter to lose weight. Well, it didn't happen just like that, and I did not say anything to her in the presence of others.

I said, "If you are going to wear that top, you need to lose a few pounds." After the student faked an illness to leave class and use the telephone, she called her mother to report my comments to her.

Needless to say, mom called me immediately and said that she did not send her daughter to school for someone to hurt her feelings and that I should apologize. I shared with mom that I did make the comment, and all the student had to do was ask me to apologize.

I was well known for having to apologize for words that should not have left my mouth. This made me realize the importance of telling the truth and teaching my students to do the same, then, if necessary, deal with the consequences.

When I would call parents to ask about students, many would tell me that the student is ill. I would always ask to speak to the student. One parent told me that her son was home ill; however, her daughter, a previous graduate, told me that her brother was in Juvenile Hall. I know I shouldn't have asked his whereabouts but was not surprised when she said, "Home, ill."

The next job was at the Naval Station and from there it was the Armed Forces Staff College. I was a substitute teacher in Virginia for a total of three days. Only elementary teachers were ill or absent, I thought, because I had to be a substitute teacher in kindergarten, fourth and fifth grades.

It was during the morning prayer, when I heard an unusual noise and looked up to see two fifth grade students' playing cards in the rear of the classroom. That was the end of my substituting career. It was during thattime that I acknowledged an unsuccessful marriage and decided to move west. I held three full time jobs in San Bernardino for more than forty years. I was at Operation Second Chance, the San Bernardino City Unified School District and currently at the San Bernardino County Superintendent of Schools Office.

Operation Second Chance gave me my first opportunity to work with young people or young adults. These students lived on the Westside of San Bernardino, and most of their dreams were nightmares. Our attempt was to provide hope for the future for them. During my second year working there, I had the opportunity to meet a school board member who learned I had a teaching credential. By then, I had abandoned all plans never to teach again.

I submitted an application, when I first arrived in California but I wasn't persistent in obtaining a job with the school system. I was encouraged to re-apply and in less than two weeks, I received a call from the Superintendent who referred me to the principal at San Bernardino High School. After I was hired, I was teased by people in the community who said, "Oh, you will be working in the prison school." I was frightened by those comments, but soon I learned that was the place I wanted to be, and the students became my friends. Many of them stay in contact and visit me from time to time.

That reminds me of my two students, who became parents during their last year of school, and started bringing their child to my house every year since she was two years old. Twelve years later, she and at least one of her parents visit me on Halloween.

Another case involves a student who married and moved to Arizona. She sends me email on a regular basis even though she graduated several years ago. It didn't take long for me to become grandmother to quite a number of young people.

One summer I worked in Santa Ana for a private, educational institution. My job was to assist students, so they could pass the GED (General Education Diploma) test. This was an adult program, so the ages of the students, ranged from eighteen to seventy. I hadn't seen a GED book, so I did the next best thing; I went to the courthouse in Orange County and took the test. After passing the first three of five tests given, I felt I had enough knowledge to make a difference. Some of my students had been out of the classroom for many years. I soon learned that you could teach older students new tricks. Strategies provided made it possible for fourteen of the seventeen students to receive their GED certificates during my tenure that summer.

I worked thirty-two years for the San Bernardino School System where I believe I have touched many lives. Unfortunately, I have attended many funerals, testified in court on behalf of students, and received collect calls from the county jail as well as state prisons.

~ Chapter Four ~

I remarried in 1979 and have been blessed with a wonderful husband.

The information provided is an encore for why I want to write a book. I feel a need to share my experiences at two middle schools, two high schools, and one District assigned position. My experiences should shed light on a wonderful segment of our society, our youth and young adults.

These incidents make me look back and wonder "How I Got Over."

Don't air your laundry in front of everyone.

"Johnny, you cannot wear that plastic cover on your head."

"Why not?"

"I said so."

"It's not bothering anyone but you."

"That's enough for you to take it off." Ten minutes later, Security brings Johnny to my office and says, "I heard you tell Johnny to keep this off his head."

"I did."

Johnny said, "The other two vice principals do not have a problem with it."

"But, I do." I responded.

He said, "So what? They did not tell me to take it off."

I became silent and do not respond. After about five minutes of being uncomfortable, Security leaves my office and leaves the student with me. I immediately close the door and say, "Don't ever question my decision in the presence of others, and since I care how you look on campus, you are not to wear that plastic cover. I did not want to embarrass you in the presence of security; however, I have a difficult time considering you a student when your head looks like it should be in the meat department of a super market." I never saw the plastic cover on his head again.

Always check for strangers, even on the bus.

Sean was having an extremely difficult time obeying the rules at school so naturally when it was time for the eighth grade field trip to Knott's Berry Farm, Sean could not attend. This was told to Sean and his father days prior to the trip. It was time to load the two buses early one Saturday morning. All the students had permission slips and were dressed appropriately. There were two chaperones on each bus because we did not want any surprises, etc.

When we arrived at the amusement park, one of the chaperones on the other bus had a look of shock, amazement, and fright. She ran towards me and said, "Sean was hiding on the bus and did not rear his head until we had passed Tyler Mall in Riverside." I remained calm and said, "Don't worry. This will probably be the worst field trip he has ever taken." We proceeded to the entrance gate where I stood and waited for Sean.

I said, "Sean, I told you that this trip would not be available to you."

"What are you going to do about it? We're already at Knott's Berry Farm."

"I'll just ask this Security Officer."

"Sir?"

"Yes,"

"This student does not have permission to be with us. Can you keep him in a safe place until I contact his father?"

"Sure, come with me, Son."

I called Sean's father who said he knew he was not suppose to get on that bus. I wondered where he was. Tell him that I am not driving that distance to pick him up. The Security Officer was glad to accommodate him until it was time to leave the amusement park. I showed some compassion by allowing him fifteen minutes to get food before we had to board the bus.

~ Chapter Five ~

When you make excuses, make sure you have a foolproof backup plan.

George had not been in school for two weeks, and when he returned, this conversation pursued. "Where have you been?" I asked. George looked at his friend and hesitated for about ten seconds and said, "I had to go to Arizona for my grandmother's funeral". "Can I reenroll in school? I said, "Sure, as soon as you bring me a copy of the funeral services". George left and while exiting the door, his friend said, "I told you, she would not believe that story."

If it looks like a duck, and if it walks like a duck, others will surely assume it is a duck.

Steve and David thought it was an excellent idea to practice gang banging on campus. They used every attempt to keep staff informed that they belong to separate gangs. They would secure their section of the cafeteria during break and managed to intimidate each other. The staff and I began taking names of the students involved in each group, and before they had an opportunity to create havoc on campus, I called them in and invited them to join my gang, which consisted of a button down dress shirt, dress slacks and a necktie. They were told they must wear the uniform for the remainder of the week. A few parents called to complain because, according to them, the students did not have dress clothes, and certainly not a necktie. I informed the parents that I would provide a shirt and necktie to each student who showed up without the proper attire. That cured the gang bashing.

If you don't use it, you lose it, except for martial arts training.

Jean and Mary were in a fight and Mary was escorted to the office by a staff member since she was the most disruptive. When talking to Jean about what led to the incident, a student yelled, "Mrs. Hill, here comes Mary!" Mary came around the corner running with great speed and definitely displayed much anger. As she approached, I move in front of Jean and threw up my arm, which caught Mary in the neck. She fell to the ground, and since it had been raining, she skidded about twelve feet. The next day, one student asked as I arrived at work, "Mrs. Hill, how is that girl doing that you karate chopped yesterday?"

"I did not karate chop anyone, I said, and you should not spread that rumor."

It appears that it was not only a message but a public service announcement, since all the students were saying that I had karate chopped a student and they should practice good behavior. I don't think there was a fight for the next few months.

Being an adult is all right if you can afford it.

Tim turned eighteen, and told his parents that he was an adult, and they were not entitled to have access to his school records, etc. Tim's mother called me and was extremely upset by her son's decision for her to, as she puts it, stay out of his business. I said, "He has a car so tell me, who pays the insurance?

She said, "I do."

I asked, "Who buys the gas?"

She said, "I do."

I asked, "Does he have a job?"

She answered, "No." I suggest that she tells him how proud she was of his manhood, and she did not need access to his school records and that she would assist him with being proud of his manhood by allowing him to pay for gas and his insurance. The next day, Tim came to school early and asked for the note back.

I asked, "Are you sure?"

He stated, "Yes, My parents have gone crazy. When they call, tell them anything they want to know."

If at first you don't succeed, try, try again, maybe?

Young Jimmy just refused to attend school and mom said I just can't make him. One day the school nurse and I decided to provide mom with a little assistance, so we drove to the house and asked for Jimmy. Jimmy's mom said he is in the bedroom but refuses to come out. We asked which room is his and started in that direction. Jimmy bolted out the door and ran towards the park. We got in the car and unfortunately, lost sight of him. We just waited because we knew a middle school student was not smarter than we were. In a matter of minutes, Jimmy appeared in the park. Thinking we had gone, Jimmy approached the sidewalk, and I said to the nurse, "There, he is". She pulls up to the sidewalk, and he tries to run from us again. By this time, two Highway Patrolmen saw us and pulled over and asked, "What's the problem." I said, "Jimmy won't attend school and we are here to make him go with us." The officers said, "Ma'am, you can't hold up traffic trying to get someone to go to school." This is quite dangerous for the two of you and the boy." I said, "But he has to go to school." The officers never got out of their car, but Jimmy yelled, "Sir, I'll go to school" and then he got in the car. That was our one-day success because I never saw Jimmy after that day.

Child abuse can be hazardous to your health.

David was smoking on campus, I instructed him to call his mother. He returned and said, "No one is home." I entered my office, called his home and got a response immediately. It was his mother who told me David had not called. I informed her that David was smoking, and either she or I could handle it. David's mom began to cry and say, "There's nothing I can do. You know if I punish him, he will call Child Protective Services on me." I said to her that I wanted proof that she was going to discipline her son and if not, I would the next day. The next morning, David entered my office holding his black eye stating, "Don't ever call my mother again. She became so angry at me; she threw her shoe and hit me in my eye. Now I have to go to work looking like this."

I apologized to David but then he said, "You know I deserved it. I will not smoke on campus again."

Some Circumstances make you a wannabe.

There were a rash of drug dealings on the middle high school campus; of course, we were in pursuit of the persons involved. One day the principal and I confronted a young man we thought was involved with drugs, and took him to her office for a search. Before searching him, we both stared at the front of his pants and knew this fourteen year old boy was ready for the world record. We looked down and then looked at him. He responded, "That's all me."

In unison, we both said, “Right”. We attempted to get the attention of the male vice principal when the student bolted out of the office, and by the time he returned to school the next day, the swelling had gone away.

As much as you want parental support, some news just isn’t worth sharing.

I had a difficult challenge with one female student but was persistent in working with the family in getting her though middle school. I insisted on a parent conference just to discover the mother had an alternative lifestyle. After pressuring mom, and her significant other about the poor attendance, the mother said, “You know we are here parents, and we are gay.”

I responded, “She still has to attend school and that’s no excuse.”

~ Chapter Six ~

What I Learned from Students that is Printable

Lesson One: All parents are not created equally

It was about 8:15 am when a student approached me.

"Hi, Mrs. Hill, I need to talk to you," said Mary who was standing in front of the school.

"Good morning, sure, let's go into my office. I'm glad to see you at school today. I haven't seen you all week." I escorted her in and motioned for her to sit down.

"That's what I want to talk about."

"You look like you are ready to cry," I said. "What is the problem?"

"My mom is strung out on cocaine and I have to watch my sisters and brother. In fact, I cannot leave home until they leave for school," she said. "That's why I've been absent so much."

"How old are they?" I asked.

"They are six, ten and eleven."

"So what do you have to do for them?"

"I have to fix breakfast, get their clothes ready and walk them to the school just down the street from my home."

"I'm glad you are doing that because you do not live in the safest neighborhood," I said.

"I know."

"Where is your mother now?"

"She's at a neighbor's house, the house where she gets her drugs."

"She hasn't been home for the past three days."

"You know I have the responsibility to reporting her to Child Protective Services."

Mary begins crying, saying, "I thought I could trust you, I'm going to take my sisters and brother, and run away. I will not let anyone split us up."

"But Mary, I have to follow the law."

"I don't care about the law. If the law was good, my mom would not be on drugs."

"I'm going to run away unless you promise me, you will not call CPS."

Lesson Two: *Child abuse or parent abuse - you decide*

I was working in my office one Thursday morning when I got a call from an elementary school principal, stating that her student came to school crying and was concerned about her sister who had been disciplined (abused) by the father. She asked if I would talk to the student. I assured her that I would. I called Jean into my office.

"Hi Jean, Did anything happen at home unusual today?" I asked.

"Yes, my father hit me with his belt."

"Why?" I asked.

"After I took my shower, I decided I did not want to come to school."

"I can understand your dad being angry, but he did not have to hit you with his belt."

Jean pulled up her shirt and said, "See. This is where he hit me."

When Jean turned with her back to me, I could see a long red area on her upper back.

"There is definitely a bruise there."

"Why was your dad so angry? Have you been at school all week?"

"No, I haven't been home."

"When were you at home last?"

"Sunday, my neighbor and her two teenage sons invited me to a birthday party at Chuck e Cheese around 3 pm, and we decided to leave the party and go to Orange County. The car broke down and we did not have a way to get home."

"How old are the boys you were with?"

"Fifteen and seventeen, their mother was with us."

"Did you call your parents to tell them what happened?"

"No."

"When did you return home?"

"This morning; about 4:30."

I was surprised that this fourteen year old student only had a slight bruise. I told the principal about the incident and stated I was having a hard time contacting Child Protective Service because had this been my child, I probably would have one less person to feed.

He said, "I know you will do what is appropriate." I had to leave campus momentarily and when I returned, I was told the police and CPS had been there.

The principal of the elementary school had called them since I had failed to do so and reported the alleged abuse. They entered the office very angrily and said they would need to conference with me on not reporting this incident but would talk to the student first. After talking to the student who gave them the same information she had given me, they left and said to my secretary, "Tell Margaret not to call us. She made a good decision."

<u>*Lesson Three:*</u> *What size has to do with it?*

One day just after lunch, two male students were about to fight just outside of my classroom. The other teachers just closed their doors. I knew if I left to call for help (I knew it was useless to ask those who closed the doors), the fight would be on. I did what I felt I was supposed to do. I stood between them and realized I had made a big mistake. Both students were over six feet tall and I am only five feet one-half inch tall. While they were arguing, I looked up and said, "I know I can't stop you from fighting but I am not moving from here. I'll just watch to see which one of you hit me first and then I will tell the principal. You know, the other day a guy hit the vice principal and he is still in jail. The vice principal is a man and here I am a woman who is asking you not to fight and you are not listening to me, so go right ahead and fight." They both looked at me and walked away.

Lesson Four: You can protect when you inspect what you expect

One day my counselor and I were standing in the front of the school waiting for the first bell to ring. It appeared to be a very calm, relaxed atmosphere where the students were talking and laughing with each other. While I was viewing it as a wonderful day, my counselor said to me, "Let's go Mrs. Hill. There is going to be a fight." Needless to say I thought she was nuts but I learned to do and asked questions later. We walked in the parking lot and met this student as she was exiting her car.

"What's going on?" my counselor asked.

"Susie was talking about me yesterday and I'm going to get her."

"Don't you think we should go in the office to talk about it?" asked my counselor.

"No. I don't like what she said and I told her I would be ready to fight today."

A conference was held with the two students and they agreed that was not the best way to settle their differences. The students exited the office and went to class. I looked at my counselor and asked, "How did you know they were going to fight?"

She said, "Gina always wears her hair hanging down and as she was getting out of the car, she put her hair in a ponytail."

Lesson Five: *A word to the wise*

I learned that students observe the behavior of adults and spread the word so others will not have to suffer any consequences. I accidentally discovered that students labeled one of my outfits as a "don't mess with me today" dress. I owned a purple dress that had big buttons on the front and long sleeves. One day while counseling a student, he said, "I should have known better after observing you in your purple dress.

"What does that have to do with your behavior?" I asked.

"We never bother you when you wear this dress because we know you are in a bad mood and the consequences for our action are always greater than other days." I waited at least two weeks before wearing that dress again and, guess what? The students all knew to leave me alone. To this day, I don't know why I sent that dress to my sister before I retired.

Lesson Six: *Big brother is watching over me*

Ed was a gang member and lived in a gang-infested neighborhood. One day, rival gang members came on campus and stared at him in a very intimidating manner. He stared back at them which intimidated me. After the non-students drove out of the parking lot, I asked Ed to come to my office. I began to rip him up one side and down the other.

"Why were you staring at them? They might have had a gun in the car."

Ed said, "I can't just stand there and not do anything. If I act a coward and someone in the group told my homies, they'd beat the hell out of me. They'd know about the confrontation by the time I got off the school bus. You just don't walk away, Mrs. Hill."

I apologized for not knowing the gang rules and told him that I worried about him often.

Lesson Seven: Let sleeping dogs lie

One student approached me and stated he was having problems with two students.

"Well George, have you had problems with them before?"

"No, it just started when John enrolled last week."

"Why were you having a problem with John." I asked.

"His brother is the one who shot me."

"He has been on campus with you for most of the year so why am I just hearing about this?"

"No one ever bothered me before." "I'm not a snitch."

Lesson Eight: Catch me if you can

Andrew and a few of his buddies felt graffiti would look terrific on the many walls, especially those in the City of Highland. Their names were known to law enforcement, but the officers could not catch them. This became a challenge to Andrew and his friends as they became even more creative with finding ways to graffiti buildings that were seven, nine and even twenty feet in the air. I informed the Mayor of Highland of these incidents and asked if the students could participate in a program that would remove them from the tagging environment. The Mayor came to school and spoke with the student and made recommendations for a more productive life. I continued to meet with Andrew to a point where he established a trusting relationship with me. "Why do you tag these buildings and billboards, Andrew?"

"It's fun, and it's a challenge."

"Don't you think it makes the city look awful," I asked?

"The city looks awful without our tagging", he responded.

"Some of the buildings I have seen your moniker on are very high and I have even seen it on a couple of billboards. How do you get up there?" "I have a video, and it shows how we access the freeway overhangs, the billboards, and the tall buildings."

"Oh really," I asked. "I sure would like to see it."

"I will admit to you that I am a tagger, but don't think I'm dumb enough to put something in your hands that you will turn over to the police." I chucked at the comment and reminded myself that trust only goes so far.

Lesson Nine: Who do you trust?

Aaron and Eddie did not care for each other, and their attitudes were as opposite as day and night. Aaron was uncommonly quiet and never bothered anyone. His home life was supremely stable with parents and older siblings working. Eddie, on the other hand, was exceptionally loud and boisterous, always threatening others including the staff members. His home life was a slight difference as his mother was a hard worker, but his father spent a few times in the county jail. One day, quiet Aaron had enough, and when Eddie asked him to meet at the corner, west of the campus, Aaron did so. A fight ensued and by the time I arrived, the sheriff officers were already at the scene. The bully, Eddie, was covered with blood on his head, face and hands while quiet Aaron was as clean as ever.

"Why were you fighting?" I asked.

"He invited me, and I felt today was as good as any to put an end to his loud talking about what he was going to do to me." Aaron responded.

Lesson Ten:Making sure that no child is left behind

School is easier for students when there are several teachers' manuals available for student use. Several teachers mentioned they had not misplaced a teacher's manual but students were turning in assignments that were completed and near perfect. These students worked diligently during the class period; however, the teachers felt they were getting outside assistance from these books. Larry would enter the office about twice a week with dozen doughnuts for the office staff. Even though, we appreciated the hospitality, we also wondered what the student was trying to cover up. After reviewing the schedule of Larry, we noted that his classes were the ones the teachers had reported on. We retrieved information on Larry from the data system and discovered his father was a high-school teacher in the district. A call was made to the father, who mentioned his son had the teacher's edition, for all the classes he had, and an additional two for classes he was planning to take. That was the end of cheating and also the doughnuts.

Lesson Eleven: *Some lessons are learned outside the classroom*

Patrick was thrilled because he had just graduated that day, and while waiting to get on the school bus, a student from another school got off the bus and began pounding away on Patrick. The other student pushed Patrick into the tree and by the time security got there, an intense fight had taken place. Mace was used to separate the boys. A parent came forward to say Larry did not start the fight and did everything to avoid a fight. The other student accused Larry of making passes at his girlfriend. Larry was cited for his involvement in the fight and was angry that he was maced when, according to him, he stopped fighting when he was instructed to do so. Larry felt this was one time he should fight for what was right, and took his case to court regarding the citation.

"Why were you fighting?"

"She told her boyfriend that I had made advances. She's not my type."

"Why didn't you tell him, you had just graduated and did not want to fight?"

"He never asked. He got off the bus and started toward me, and I backed away until I hit the tree and had no other choice but to defend myself." "You know I like to fight but this time I was not bothering anyone. I was just waiting for my bus."

"I know. A woman got out of her car, to state you were innocent."

"You need to know that usually when you are doing the right thing, you will have witnesses and people who are not afraid to speak in your behalf."

"I'm glad the parent stopped to tell you what happened." he said.

A ticket was issued to Larry even though I recommend that I thought that was not appropriate. The case went to court, and Larry won.

Lesson Twelve: *Some banks are where you find the money*

Raymond was an outstanding student but enjoyed bugging his teachers for restroom passes. This day was no different, and when a teacher reported that her purse had been taken from the classroom, a search immediately began. The purse was located on the stair steps near the fire escape, and the only contents missing were forty dollars. There weren't any students in the hallway at that time, but I asked the teacher in a close by classroom if she had given a student a pass. I asked the student about the purse, and the student indicated it was not there when she was out of class. The only person she saw out of class was Raymond. I entered Raymond's classroom, but he was not there. His teacher said he asked for a pass but never returned. I radioed security and asked her to meet me in the parking lot. We got in my car and drove to MacDonald's, the closest place that I felt I would find students. There was Raymond and three other boys eating hamburgers, fries, etc. I escorted Raymond out of the restaurant and searched him as he stood near the door. He still had more than twenty dollars in his pocket. "Where did you get this money from?" I asked.

"I got it cutting lawns and from my dad for my weekly allowance."

"I don't believe you. Did you take a teacher's purse from the classroom?"

"No, I just told you where I got the money from."

"I'm taking the rest of this until I validate your story."

I drove to Raymond's house and stopped his father from working. He was painting the exterior of the house. "Good morning, I'm sorry to bother you, but Raymond was truant and at MacDonald's. How much money should he have?" His father responded, "I don't think he should have had any. I asked him to help me around the house, and he refused so I didn't give him any money all week." "He was in possession of $40 before he and three other boys went to eat. He said it was partial allowance and cutting the neighbor's lawn last weekend." "I'm sure you're right. Neither his mother nor I gave him any money."

Lesson Thirteen: Smokey the Bear didn't take the day off

Robert decided he was old enough to smoke while he attended middle school. His mother was not convinced he was a smoker, so we knew we had to provide convincing evidence to her. One day Robert decided to leave school without permission and wait for his friends to leave school for the day. He went to an undeveloped area near the campus, and I assumed he was lighting a cigarette, when the area that had many dried weeds caught fire. He ran to school to report the fire but stated he did not know how it started. The fire engines arrived in time to save his jacket and notebook. This student is now an attorney.

Lesson Fourteen: It's a family affair

The apple does not fall far from the tree. Monique had musical talent and loved to play the guitar and sing. She would get sent to the office most days for being under the influence of marijuana. After months and months of counseling, the marijuana use continued. A conference was held with Monique and her mother. After a few rounds of getting nowhere, Monique's mom said she needs to tell us something confidential.

She stated, "I need you to know that marijuana is acceptable in my home. Monique, her brother, her father and I smoke it on a regular basis. I knew that I could not change the behavior of this beautiful, intellectual young lady, so my request was for her not smoke because it was illegal but if she continued to smoke marijuana, please do so before taking her shower and then come to school but do not smoke after she dressed for the day; otherwise, she would need to stay home. I thought it was a good solution, but the student dropped out of school.

Lesson Fifteen: *I was my brother's keeper*

Kenneth was an exceptionally nice young man who was always polite and neatly dressed. He rode the bus to school and came from a neighborhood where the economic situation was less than wealthy. I would tease him often about being a model for students and that even though you lived in the ghetto; you could dress like a student from Beverly Hills. He would chuckle and move on. Kenneth would skip school two to three days at a time during each month and always had an explanation that was reasonable and believable. One day after school we had this conversation: "Now Kenneth, tell me, what are you really doing when you miss school two or three days at a time?"

"It won't happen again, I promise you."

"What were you doing that has come to a halt?"

"I was a coyote runner. I would pick up illegal immigrants at the border near Calexico and transport them to the Los Angeles area."

"You know that is illegal, and you could go to jail for a long time." I stated.

"I'm lucky. Last week while making a run, the police stopped me near Indio and took my truck. They said if they caught me again, they would take me to jail."

"You should count your blessings since they did not take you to jail then."

"I know. They left me on the side of the road, and I had to hitchhike home."

"What is sad is I used all the money I made on clothes and didn't even buy a car."

Lesson Sixteen: If you hang with the eagles you will soar like an eagle

I delivered keys to a local church when I was approached by one of the volunteers who said, "Margaret Hill, you don't remember me but I sure appreciated what you did for my son when you were at the middle School." After giving me her son's name, I said, "I remember your son, he was such a nice young man."

"What is he doing now?"

"He's an attorney." She responded.

I asked about his friends, and as I called off each name, I heard such things as, he's a doctor, he's an attorney, he owns a business, etc. Speaking of no child left behind, this is living proof of what can occur when students encourage each other.

Lesson Seventeen: Many may stumble but some never fall

Ken and Bobbie were students who were co-habitating and lived across the street from the school. They were arguing in a classroom, and the teacher sent them to me for a resolution to their conflict. The young woman was crying, and the young man was still yelling at her when they entered my office.

"What's wrong?" I asked.

"He's angry because I was talking on the telephone last night and wouldn't tell him who I was talking with."

"Why do you need to know Ken?" I asked.

"She was probably talking with some guy. She knows I don't allow that."

"Well you need to realize that you're not her father."

"So what? We are living together."

"So what is correct, I stated. "Perhaps you should move if you can't allow her to have her freedom." "I'm not moving, and she's not going to talk to anyone she wants to."

"That makes you the big man, not in charge of anything, doesn't it?" I stated. "I don't have to listen to either of you."

Ken stormed out of my office, crossed the street and jumped the fence. I asked Bobbie where he was going. She said he is going to my house and tell my father about our argument. Bobbie cried harder and louder stating, "My dad always takes his side." I asked for her phone number and immediately called the house. Her father answered. "Mr. Jones? Ken just stormed out of my office, and is on his way home. I need your support on this one. Please let him know that you are Bobbie's father, and he has no right to monitor her calls. He should be walking in the door any minute now."

"Okay, Mrs. Hill, I'll tell him."

In less than five minutes, Ken returned to school, came to my office and apologized. I explained to him the best way to be a respectable man and maintain his dignity. Ken is now in the navy, married to Bobbie, and they have two beautiful children.

~ Chapter Seven ~

It's Not Always what you know, But Accepting ....What you don't Know and Moving Forward

I was raised on the farm and was remarkably talented at learning what I heard others say. I certainly did not invent Ebonics; however, I could have easily taken the first place trophy annually. It was not unusual for me to say the following when I was young and living on the farm. (These are the ones I remembered): "You is gonna do what?"

"He be's the boy I like."

"I ain't gonna help you with that."

"They done gone to town."

"Chunk the ball to me, I can catchit."

"I sho' does like this candy."

Now that I'm older, I often wonder what happened to many of the sharecroppers and their families as we all spoke the same. We did not invent the English language nor were our forefathers allowed to read, so did we have something good going on and didn't know it? I didn't have as many problems communicating in the south with those with little or no education as I do with some on the west coast who are fluent English speakers. When I first arrived in California, and someone would correct my grammar, especially in public, I wanted to say, "If you understand me, what's the big deal."

I feel that all people want to be accepted, and recognized as proficient English speakers; however, I learned from students that communicating is more valuable than proper communication. The non-verbal communication resulted in a number of students not being successful. It was not unusual to see groups of students mad-dogging each other. Most of this came about due to an issue in the community. One student, who was training to become a golden glove boxer, broke the handcuffs and continued his aggressiveness. Another student would walk around campus with the water cover in one hand. That thing weighed about twenty pounds. My non-verbal communication was observed when I got in trouble for chasing my cousin around the heater in the classroom while I had a baseball bat in my hand because he'd made me angry.

I don't remember any of my teachers speaking the way I did, but no one told me I was wrong in my assembly of words. It was just the farm mentality; however, when I got to high school, I can remember my shorthand teachers saying, "You need to learn how to speak correct English before you consider going to college." I was exceptionally skilled at shorthand, so I said, "She doesn't know what she is talking about. I will go to school and become a secretary."

When I got to college, I did not do well at all. My English grades were awful, and I only got decent grades in typing and shorthand. In fact, I was placed on academic probation the first year, and that led me to believe I just was not college material. I located a job working as a shampoo girl by looking in the yellow pages. My next job was working as a file clerk in a real estate office. My boss often told me that I would need to improve my English skills, and I was easily convinced after I had to retype just about everything he gave me. I worked with a group of terrific people, and they gave me all the support that I needed to complete the tasks at hand. I didn't have to use any writing skills at the bank, and by the time I got the civil service job and was working at the Armed Forces Staff College, I'd gotten somewhat better and would do all the written correspondence for the Lieutenant that I worked for. Even today, I look back and wonder how I got over.

My first job in San Bernardino was working at Operation Second Chance. I can still remember a ten-page document I looked at and said to myself, “They sure did misspell barrier a lot. I need to change this.” Of course, I did not know the culture of the State but I knew how to type. I took this document and planned to perfect it by changing “barrios” to “barriers.” Then I was gutsy enough to make several copies and tossed out the old ones. My supervisor never said anything but now, as I think about it, I’m sure they had a big laugh and wanted to know why did they hire me. No one ever told me that I’d done anything wrong. Even with all of that, I got a job with the San Bernardino City Unified School District. You know why? I could type and was proficient at shorthand.

My models were the teachers and staff members that I worked with. This coaching continued until the day I retired. I would always ask teachers to critique my work, including the publication, “A True Alternative” in the Association of California School Administrators Leadership Magazine. I listened to them and I learned from them. They coached and helped me become a success.

All of this is significant because I used my lack of a standard education to assist the young people who entered my life for nearly forty years. When students shared their work, I would first comment, “That is very creative, however, you must make your corrections.” I would follow-up with, “Why don’t you let me help you.” It was not unusual for me to say to students, “You are so brilliant, but people will judge you by the way you spell and what you write. Your syntax is excellent, so we just have to work on the spelling.”

There are some merits to being a poor speller especially if you are having disciplinary problems. At one of the middle schools, a student wrote on the restroom wall, “Mrs. Hill is a b------. She has no creadibility (sic).”

I had a problem with a female student just before the lunch break and had given her a stern reprimand but did not suspend her. So naturally, she was the first one I was going after. I found the classroom where this student was and asked the teacher if I could give the students an assignment. I told the students that I wanted the principal to see how well they could write and if they would each take out a sheet of paper and write the statement that I was going to read to them.

They all complied. I read, "The principal is the best person for this school because of her credibility."

I collected the papers and read them in my office. The student that I was certain had written on the wall was the one who spelled "credibility" incorrectly. When I confronted her, she admitted what she had done.

Mary was not the target, but when young men came by looking for her brothers and began yelling, she and her mother went outside the home to see what was going on. One of the guys opened fire and Mary was hit.

I didn't look forward to the hospital visit, but when I entered the room, Mary asked, "Are we still having a prom?"

God takes the good ones early sometimes. David had a bad heart and knew he did not have long to live. His one dream was to obtain a high-school diploma which he acquired in June. David passed away in July.

Frank shot himself in the head and was transported to the local hospital. I was unaware of who had been injured until I received a call at home from one of the staff members. I immediately rushed to the hospital where several students were waiting and crying in the waiting room. Frank's mother came out to greet us and said it was just a matter of time before they pulled the plug. Frank was not going to make it. Frank's mother did not want students to see her son in this condition, but then she agreed to honor the request. As the students entered the room, one of them grabbed my hand and said, "You need to go with us." Frank's physical condition is imbedded in my memory. A memorial service was held on campus for this young man.

One very handsome young man was very involved with school activities and student council. He was seem most days walking around campus with a Bible in his hand. He was a peace builder and students respected him as a student and a leader. After graduation, he enlisted in the Navy and was stationed nearby. He was also a good son so one weekday morning, while returning to the Naval Base after purchasing a vehicle for his mother, he was in an automobile accident which took his life.

When I was a teacher at the traditional high school, I became very acquainted with one of my instructional aides. We played tennis, softball and just socialized on several occasions. She and her husband stopped by one day after attending the funeral of a friend who'd been killed in an automobile accident. The friend was driving a corvette, and we had a corvette also. They begged us not to drive it again because of the death of their best friend, and they felt the car just was not safe. During the next six months, they were both killed by a wrong-way driver on the freeway.

~ Chapter Eight ~

These tragedies affected how I work with our youth. Some are dreams, many are nightmares. A lifetime of pain is due to a few minutes of joy. I noticed George standing near the custodian's truck, and he was keeping a watchful eye on me. I parked my body on the brick planter and remained there until five minutes before the lunch period was over.

Assuming students only had time to get ready for class, I entered my office and prepared for the after lunch assistance when I heard someone kick my door hard. They said, "Mrs. Hill, there's been an accident and students are all over the road." Several of the teachers, and I ran to the scene of the accident to see a truck that belonged to the custodian turned upside down and six or seven bodies lying still on the ground. The driver of the truck was walking around in a daze.

I later discovered that when I went to the office, the students had made a mad dash to jump in the truck and go to the local store. In their haste to get there and back before the next class period started, George had accelerated his speed and lost control of the vehicle. There were six or seven girls riding in the back of the truck and they were all thrown out. Fortunately, all students survived. Channel Four television station and the local newspaper provided media cover of this event that left me sad, and wondering if I had the courage to carry on had one of the students failed to survive this awful accident.

Sometimes the innocent get punished. It was not unusual for Craig to be identified with a group of students who were creating unrest. He always managed to be on the surface and usually did not get punished because I was not able to catch him. After he graduated from high school, he continued to be "just there" when the action was going on. One night while trying to protect a young lady from domestic abuse, he was murdered. This time, unfortunately, he was doing the right thing.

~ Chapter Nine ~

Maggie's Kids Foundation

I start my career at San Andreas High School in July 1987 under very scary circumstances. I had been informed this is the school where you send students who did not comply with the expectations in the traditional high school. I never heard anyone talk about the success of these students nor did I hear anyone talk about the teachers. So, you see, it was easy to believe the teachers and students who went to San Andreas were similar to going to the Twilight Zone and never heard from again. I've always wanted to know what you need to know to get a job, but I certainly did not expect to attain the principal's position at San Andreas. When I was notified that I would be principal of the school, I said, "Oh no. That's where I sent all the students who had given me grief."

It did not take long for the love affair to begin. Those students were wonderful even though many of them had major challenges. They were terrific citizens who had just been swept aside for "those students" who wanted to get an education without disruptions.

The pain of these students was shared by all of us. One day I shared the names and the number of students who were homeless but found a haven at San Andreas. One teacher convinced me that I need to have a foundation to support the needs of these students. I knew I had to leave a legacy so in order to start this foundation, I decided that, instead of retirement gifts and proclamations, I would ask that donations be made to Maggie's Kids Foundation. I guess I should tell you how Maggie came about. The students who were involved in an entrepreneurship program had an opportunity to launch a café and wanted to name it after me; however, they felt Margaret was not sporty enough, so they asked me if I would allow them to name the café "Maggie." I was honored.

The community and staff supported my vision for the foundation and gave unselfishly to the foundation. I hope one day that enough funds will be available to provide a dormitory or an alumni house for homeless students. I must have encountered at least twenty students who did not know where they would sleep that night, or where they would get their next meal once the school was closed for the day.

This incident occurred early one Monday morning.

"Mrs. Hill, I need to talk to you," said Don.

"Of course, come to my office," I said.

"Have a seat."

"You will never guess what happened to me."

"You look good and well rested. It couldn't have been that bad."

"When I got home Friday, I asked my mom if I could spend the night with my friend. She said yes, so I put a few things in a bag and went to my friend's house. Everything was fine until I returned home this morning to get clean clothes for school."

"What happened? I asked.

"My mother moved to New York and didn't tell me."

A student always came to school wearing a long trench coat daily. Of course, I felt he was a drug pusher. I shared with the School Police that I wanted a random check and identified this student as one to be checked. They complied but only found a cell phone on this student which they confiscated and gave to me. The student was allowed to come to the office to share why he was bringing a cell phone to school.

"I have to have that phone." he said.

"Why? I asked.

"It's the only way I can get in touch with my boss. He gave me this cell phone so that he can call me to work when there is an emergency."

"Why don't you leave the phone at home until school is out?" I asked.

"I do not have a home."

"I'm sure that's your own choosing. How can I get in touch with your parents?"

"When you get in touch with them, let me know." he said.

"I haven't heard from my parents in over a year."

"Where do you keep your things while you are at school?" I asked.

"I have on everything that I own. I wash my clothes every night."

Another student dropped out of school during his senior year because he was homeless. His mother owned a vehicle, so they were able to park the car in a vacant lot which became their home at night.

~ Chapter Ten ~

The Community

I became involved in the San Bernardino Black Culture Foundation during Black History month in 1986. The biggest project for this organization was organizing and supporting a parade that was held the first Saturday in February. All members of this group are volunteers, and numerous hours were spent preparing for this televised event.

During my reign as president in 2002, I recommended that we consider moving the parade to the center of the city so that all communities could come together to enjoy this event. A few volunteers were supportive but suggested that we entertain the move the following year.

In October, 2003, we voted and decided to make the move. This caused many of the citizens in what was previously known as the predominantly African-American community to become alarmed about moving the parade from home it had known for the past twenty plus years. The suggestion to move the parade had been an issue almost every year since 1986, but the fuse was quickly extinguished and business continued as usual.

I always stressed to my students that sometimes when you step out on the limb of change, you might go alone or you might have a few followers, but very seldom do you have the support of everyone. Therefore, when you do this, make sure you support your vision for change. These students were encouraged to use whatever creativity to support their vision of success.

Brad was not the most diligent person in turning in his assignments. In fact, I'm not sure he did more than show up daily with a respectful attitude and a desire to coordinate the displays in the school's business department. This student opened a floral business and has been one of the decorators for the U. S. President's Inaugural Ball for four of the past five elections.

This student refused to participate in a project assignment. I told him of his options, and he decided to stage a fashion show for the entire school. This event was remarkably successful and became a ritual of that school for the next few years.

A student was reviewing his portfolio of dress designs in his class one day when he was encouraged by the staff to do a senior project. His formal designs were submitted for the First Lady, and his was one of the three selected throughout the United States.

These are several of the success stories when you are not afraid to take a step out on the limb. They gave me the courage to support moving the parade where all segments of the community could enjoy instead of those who lived in one part of the city.

~ Chapter Eleven ~

Being Creative with my Age

I was born December 17, 1940, I think. My birth certificate states I was born December 19 in Southampton County. I always celebrate on the 17th, the day my mother told me I was born. It was not unusual, I understand for a birth certificate to be a day or two late getting recorded. On the bottom of my birth certificate, it reads, "When six to nine months old have your doctor give the baby toxoid to prevent diphtheria." For all family members interested in the family tree and should I become deceased prior to my book becoming famous, I am listed with the State Registrar of Vital Statistics at Richmond, Virginia, Vol. 3384, and No.53354.

The most devastating time in my life occurred in 1966 when my mother, at age 54, and my niece, age 4, transitioned within two days of each other. My mother had cancer and was diabetic. She did not share her illnesses with us. In fact, I did not know she was diabetic until her death, and since I was the one selected to be at the hospital with her, the doctor gave me the terrible news. I'm not sure either of these illnesses took my mother away from this earth. My four year-old niece was hit by a truck driver the day before. Karen's tragic death was in the newspaper and on the radio news. When my mother awakened on the morning after the accident, the radio was removed from her room, and she was not allowed to read the newspaper. She knew something was wrong. That was confirmed when my sister who resided in New York and I visited her later that day. The great news is December was the month I received my Master's and Administrative degrees. The other good news is this was the month my divorce became final from my first husband.

The seventeen will represent the number of bad experiences during my lifetime that I'm willing to share in this book.

~ *Bad Experiences* ~

There are bad experiences already mentioned and will not be repeated.

1. I saw my life pass before my eyes about 9:28 pm on a Wednesday. While in college, we were always eager to go to the USO hall to listen to the music and dance with the military men. We had to be inside the dance hall by 9:30 pm and this particular night, the bus was late dropping my friends and me off. We had to cross Tidewater Drive which was six lanes of highway. We ran across five traffic lanes, but by the time we reached the sixth, I fell in the middle of the street. I saw the many car lights and heard my friends crying, "Please Margaret, get up." I managed to do so and narrowly escape death.

2. I was a bank teller and at work when I saw these men come in with extraordinarily conservative suits. They walked with the branch manager to his office and then returned to remove the man who was working as a teller next to me. At the end, of the work day, we were told they were from the FBI and we could not leave. We were allowed to relax in the staff lounge. This conversation ensued.
   "Why do you think they are here?"
   "I don't know. Money is missing." I said.
   "I wonder how much?"
   "Probably $10, 000," I said.
   "Wow! That's a lot."
   "It sure is," I said.

We were enjoying a light snack when one of the men entered the room, and said they would be interviewing us and called my name first. Of course, I was thinking, "That's right. Call on the one Black employee first."

I was asked if I knew the money was missing, and I said I felt the only reason they were here was the loss of money.
They asked if I knew how much and I stated, "No."

The shocker was when I was asked why I thought $10,000 was missing. I became extremely paranoid since I was working in the teller cage next to where the money was missing.

I agreed to take a polygraph test which was administered about two weeks later. A year later, the bank next door to the real estate office where I was working part-time was robbed. One of the former FBI employees was investigating, and when he came to the office to ask if we had seen anything, he focused his eyes on me for at least thirty seconds. I said to myself, "Here we go again." He did not interrogate me, however.

Three years later, I applied for a job with the FBI and had completed all the paperwork when I got a call for a personal interview. The representative looked at me when I walked in the office said, "Oh, you were at the bank when the money came up missing." That was the beginning and end of my interview.

3. I was taking a class at Old Dominion University where I had a professor who felt Blacks were of a different breed. She would always talk about issues and give the Black perspective. The students would look at me out of pity, I believe, but did not say anything. I did not say anything because I knew it would affect my grade. For example, she said Blacks think lettuce is cabbage. I also remember her stating that Blacks did not get a good education in their schools because Black teachers did not have the same education. She even gave us symbols representing alphabets, and we had to read a sentence with these symbols. We read so slowly that it was comical, but then she said, "That's how our Black students read." It was embarrassing to me because I was the only black student in the class and felt if all teachers at the Old Dominion University felt that way about students who were not white, I did not ever want to become a teacher.

4. When one door closes, usually another one opens. My supervisor at the bank was a retired admiral who did not have a problem saying what was on his mind whether it hurt your feelings or not. When he recommended that I test for management, I was so amazed because my supervisor always said what was on his mind and I know he would not have recommended me unless he felt I met the qualifications. There was an orientation meeting where the nine of us met on a Saturday before taking the day-long test. We were told that there were only three positions, and we would be called in for a post test interview to learn of our standings. At the end, of the day, we all talked about such a stressful test, and only three of us completed all sections. I was one of the three and felt happy about our conversation as I drove home. When the test results came back, my supervisor called me into his office and told me that he was sorry that I did not make it. He shared his disappointment and suggested that I follow up with the interview, insisting that I get the reason I was not selected. My heart was heavy and I was prepared to accept the results until they told me, we would not review any of the tests, and that if there had been one more position, I would have received it. The three who were selected were men, and I knew then it was more my gender than the color of my skin. I was terribly disappointed but, I did not lose my self-confidence. My supervisor supported my decision to look for another job.

5. Bob and I made several attempts to get married in 1978 and 1979, but it seemed as though it was not meant to be. Every weekend that we were supposed to go to Las Vegas to tie the knot, one of us got sick. In May 1979, we said we were going to get married no matter what and had shared that with the family. My niece, Erika, called me the morning of May 26 and suggested that we take our cars to her parents' home to wash. I thought it was a good idea since Bob was at work, and we still had time on our hands before the departure. Erika got to her parents house first, but neither of them were home--just her sister, Christina and brother, Raymond was there. When I drove up, I saw a strange car in front of the house, and Erika ran to my car stating, "Diana is dead." Diana is Erika's sister who had recently celebrated her sixteenth birthday. I said, "No way. How do you know?" She said, "This man is from the Coroner's office and he said so." I went to the man and asked, "Are you sure Diana is the one dead?" He did not respond but instead put his hand in his pocket and took out a picture so that I could see it. To me, that was the day the earth stood still. Diana had encountered so many obstacles, that I felt she was cheated out of a professional skating championship as she was one of the best I had ever seen perform. Unfortunately, what we did not want to know was the truth. I said, "No way are we going to Las Vegas." "We need to be with the family." My brother, Kenneth, and sister-in-law, Mamie, said, "Please go. Do it for Diana."

6. We went to Las Vegas and got married. Every year when we celebrate our anniversary, we always remember Diana. George did not care much about school, neither did his brother. They were habitually truant and one could always smell smoke on them. They did not have family support even though a father and mother were in the home. One day I witnessed George smoking and began my reprimand. "Why are you smoking on campus?"

"Because we could smoke before you came here."

"It was legal then. As of January 1, the law was changed."

"That's stupid."

"Perhaps but law is law."

"And, of course, you are going to enforce it?"

"You bet."

"If I catch you smoking again, I will transfer you to Adult Education." There was a long, very long stare. George said, "I am so angry at you right now, I feel like hitting you." "You better make the first hit your best shot", I responded. George left the office and I never saw him again until one year later when I had a flat tire near this tire repair shop. George smiled and said, "Don't worry Mrs. Hill; I'll take care of your tire." He did.

7. Don was in love with his high school sweetheart. He was not as successful as she so while he was still trying to get a high-school diploma, she was in college. One day while in my office, we discussed this relationship. "Don't you think Mary has outgrown you?" "No, Mrs. Hill. She cares for me."

"Usually people adapt, and associate with those who share the same intellect. She is in college and you are still in high school."

"So what? We will always be together."

"What will you do when she tells you that her interest in you is no longer there?"
"I will kill myself if my girlfriend leaves me."
"Don't say that."
A few months passed and I grabbed my newspaper to read after spending a week out of state. I was quite surprised, if not shocked, when I read Don's obituary. He had severed his relationship with Mary.

8. Middle school students spend a lot of energy developing strategies to keep others from liking them. I lived within two blocks of the school where I was working. This was true for about eight of my students. Jim would run home at the end of the school day, put his dogs on leashes and wait for other students to walk by and then scare them with the dogs. After a few months, the neighborhood boys had enough. They threatened to beat Jim and injury his dogs. His mother was concerned for his safety when he went to school because she left for work first. Jim said, "Don't let them hurt me, Mrs. Hill." I agreed to walk him to school daily but in order for him to maintain dignity, I called him on the telephone when I was ready to walk out the door. The other students were waiting for him and used a few explicits when they saw me. These students did not know that our trek to school was planned.

9. Robert and Bill were horsing around in class one afternoon in lieu of doing class work. There was a discussion about who should be in control of the backpack. The ongoing saga was heard by the teacher who escorted both students to my office.
"What's in the backpack?
"Nothing."

"Why did this discussion regarding the backpack linger on?"

"I don't know."

"I will check it now so give it to me."

"Okay."

"Don't tell me this is a gun?

"It's a gun."

I retrieved the gun and backpack, and then called school police. When they arrived, the students were arrested and taken to Juvenile Hall.

10. While teaching at the traditional high school, I became concerned about a student who had excellent attendance prior to this time. Telephone calls were made but no one on campus had knowledge the student was in juvenile Hall. When the student returned to school, he shared with me what had happened.

"Where have you been?" I asked.

"Juvenile Hall."

"Why?"

"I got caught breaking into a tuxedo store."

"That was not a smart thing to do."

"It was the first time."

"First time?" I asked.

This is what happened. My friend and I went to do the robbery and to enter, we broke the front plate glass, crawled in and grabbed a few tuxedos. We left, went home and crawled in bed. We talked about how easy it was so we got up, dressed, and decided to return to the same store. As soon as we entered the broken window, one piece of glass fell and set off the alarm. The police were there in seconds. The judge gave us six months.

11. It was not unusual for parents, who were also employees of the

District, to enroll these sixteen and older children into San Andreas. Susan was an employee and

Katherine, her daughter, was a student. Katherine's boyfriend was also a student there. One day Katherine came in, somewhat upset.
"What's wrong?" I asked.
"My boyfriend and I just broke up and now he is my mom's boyfriend."

12. The student was having a difficult time controlling her anger in the special education class. She was told she would probably be issued a suspension after talking to me. "What's happening to you lately, Marion?"
"I don't know. I guess I just want to be left alone."
"You know that it's hard to do when you are in the classroom with a lot of students and then the teacher has an expectation of you also."
"I know and I know better."
"Thanks for accepting responsibility for your actions, I said.
"I need to get you off campus for the remaining of the day but you can come back tomorrow." Marion said thanks and then took a small pocketknife from her purse and began cleaning her fingernails.

"What are you doing with that knife?" I asked.

"I use this knife to clean my fingernails."

"Knives are not allowed at school. You know that."

"I do, Mrs. Hill, but I was only going to clean my nails.

13. Unless I could smell the drug or alcohol, I had a difficult time making a diagnosis. Carrie said, "I don't feel good. Can I go home?"
"Well, school has not started yet so you may. Please call me as soon as you get home."
As soon as the truck pulled off, one student ran into my office shouting, "What are you doing, Mrs. Hill?"
"Why did you let her leave?"

"Couldn't you tell she was under the influence of a controlled substance?"
I responded, "No", and then called her mother.

14. Ken and George came on campus tardy and appeared to be under the influence of alcohol. I immediately ushered them into my office and asked, "What have you been drinking?" "Nothing, Mrs. Hill," they replied.

"What do you have in your pockets?"

"Nothing."

"I need to check for myself. Do I have your permission?"

"Yes."

"Why do you have these beer caps in your pockets?"

"We found them."

"Did you come to school alone?"

No, Richard was with us." I left the two students in my office, and escorted Richard from his classroom to the office. I was not able to detect the smell of alcohol on him. "Were you with Ken and George this morning?" I asked. "Yes, we came to school together. We were late though."

"Did you go with them to the store this morning?"

"Yes. We were together."

"Why didn't they give you some of the alcohol they purchased?"

"They know I have an ulcer and cannot drink."

Ken and George were not aware that Richard had just validated what I had witnessed. I called Ken's grandmother and George's mother, and then I called school police. I further notified them of their suspension. I overhead Ken whisper to George, "I sure hope the police gets here before my grandmother." He was not lucky with his request.

15. One of my responsibilities as vice principal was to get and keep students on campus. I observed five students entering an automobile after the beginning of Period One. I asked the Campus Resource Officer to get in the car so that we can get those students back on campus. We chased the students on surface streets and then on the freeway. We pulled our car near them and asked the driver to pull over and stop the car. The driver complied. I exited my car and went to the driver's window and I was informed by several of the students in the car that I was not a Highway Patrolman. I reminded them that if they were not at school and in my office before I returned to school, their punishment would be greater than a ticket. They were patiently waiting when I returned to school.

16. Tamika decided this was a good time to commit suicide. She lived with her biological mother and father but had become upset at her father when he disciplined her about her bad behavior on the school bus and her action regarding her curfew. Tamika returned to school and I requested that she meets with me for a personal conference. We discussed the decision she made to not end her life and she also made a commitment not to every consider suicide again.

I asked, "Do you know how much it cost for a funeral?"

"No", she replied.

"What do you think it cost?"

"Maybe $500."

I reminded here that I had lost my sister and the funeral expenses were in excess of $5000 and that was just a basic funeral.

"Do you realize that if you die, your father will have to take time away from his job and will not be able to feed or pay rent?"

"No, I never thought of that."

"Do you have grandparents?"

"Yes, some in Pennsylvania and some in Texas."

"Don't you think they will want to be at your funeral?"
"Yes".
"They won't have time to drive here because both states are more than one thousand miles away which means they will need airline reservations."
"I never thought of that".
"Who will pick them up from the airport?"
"I don't know because my dad does not have a car."
"Where are they going to stay when they get here?"
"I don't know."
"Now that you know what this will do to your family financially, what are you going to do the next time you get upset and depressed?"
"I didn't know committing suicide could be so expensive so I guess I have to think of something else."

17. Charles was a very good looking young man who could charm a snake without getting bit. He was well dressed and very popular with the male and female students. I was informed that Charles might be selling drugs on campus. He was so smooth with his actions that it was difficult for me to catch him doing anything wrong. Not to be outdone, I chose my mission which was to shadow Charles the entire time he was on campus. I would stand in front of the school until he arrived, and then followed him until he got to his first period class. When it was time for dismissal, I would be standing outside his classroom door and kept an eye on him during his fifteen minute break. I would walk behind him to his next class and continued this cycle throughout the day until school was dismissed. After a few days of obviously following Charles, he asked, "Why are you following me, Mrs. Hill?"

"I heard you are a drug pusher and I want to prove them wrong."
"You don't have to follow me around campus."
"I know, but I want to let everyone know they have identified the wrong person."
"It is embarrassing to have you follow me."
"I owe it to you and I know one day you will thank me."
Charles transferred to another school to complete his high school diploma. I wished him well.

~ Chapter Twelve ~

Rewarding Experiences

I am so grateful for a full, abundant life that as I talk about these rewarding experiences and recognitions, I've attached my personal quote to each.

1. I received a telephone call late one Sunday regarding the Underground Railroad. The coordinator asked, "Do you know anyone who wants to take this educational trip? We had two last minute cancellations and the trip is scheduled for next Saturday. I said, "Sure. I want to go." The school district administrator approved my request which gave me an opportunity to travel from Ohio, down to Kentucky, back to Ohio, then to Canada, down to Michigan and back to Ohio. Visiting the home of Harriet Beecher Stowe, walking on the site where Topsy, who was featured in Uncle Tom's Cabin, lived, and touring the original Uncle Tom Cabin meant a lot to me. I also visited safe houses for those enslaved and witnessed the auction blocks, shackles, sleeping quarters, etc. I learned to appreciate the strength of Harriet Tubman and her great deeds, especially when I participated in a reenactment of being chased by slave owners and dogs, trying to escape to freedom while touring the Walls Museum in Canada.

"Give thanks to the past, appreciate the present, and leave a legacy for the future"

2. I received a call from Sacramento stating I have been recommended to attend an educational summit conference hosted by Speaker of the House, Willie Brown. I was one of the panelists who were given the opportunity to say positive things about our students. I also met the "Teacher of the Year" who, at that time, would drive around San Diego and pick up homeless students to provide an education to them.

"You don't always need a silver spoon. Some things should be allowed to fall out of the bowl"

3. I participated in a few demonstrations in 1957 while a student at Norfolk State College. Several schools had closed to avoid integration and several companies had not embraced diversity. I was asked to apply for a job with Virginia National Bank because they did not have any minority bank employees. I applied, was accepted, and was told that I became the first African American to work as a bank teller in the State of Virginia. This was the assurance that since I received that equal opportunity, it would prevail in Virginia and it was the first time that I realized that sit-ins, demonstrations, and fighting segregation had paid off.

"There isn't a good place in society for those who give up"

4. I was elated when I received the District area Educator Options Administrator of the Year award and certainly moved beyond tears to receive the same award for the State of California. As a result of this award, I was invited to write an article for the "*Leadership Magazine*," a publication for members of the Association of California School Administrators. My article, "*A True Alternative*," focused on the attitudes of

students, parents, and staff in making an alternative school effective.

"How others see you is how you should see yourself so you can be your best"

5. I had the opportunity to interview James Meredith, the first Black to enter the University of Mississippi. This was to be my first fifteen-minute interview for television but as I got involved with his life as a fighter for civil rights, the fifteen minutes extended into a one-hour show. Mr. Meredith was just as surprised as I was that the interview was lengthy. This was my first interview and it led to several others such as the on-site interview for the City of Highland in 2003 and the Civil War Re-enactment in Calico in 2004.

"Having the desire to make a difference is half the battle"

6. I received the Black Rose Award from the San Bernardino Black Culture Foundation. These awards are given to unsung heroes for their involvement in community work. This resulted in my position as announcer for the Annual Black History Parade, televised often during the month of February on the local access television station for San Bernardino, Riverside, and Los Angeles Counties.

"It doesn't matter what you do, just do something to make a positive difference"

7. I was selected by the City of Highland to be the Grand Marshal in the Fourth of July parade. This honor came about because of my involvement with the chartering of the Highland Family YMCA and the community clean up that was done for citizens of the city.

"Are you willing to give or willing to get"

8. I received the Pioneer Award from the NAACP for dedication and commitment to the community. This award is given to individuals who have demonstrated a level of commitment to the community including education, law enforcement, and spirituality.

"Thinking you can is all you need"

9. I received the Golden Apple Award which is sponsored by the San Bernardino Education Round Table. This is a collaboration of the San Bernardino City Unified School District, San Bernardino Valley College, and California State University, San Bernardino. This award is in recognition of outstanding services to students.

"Row, row, row your own boat"

10. I was selected to be "Woman of the Year" by Assemblyman John Longville, a Democrat, and two weeks later, I received a call inviting me to be "Woman of the Year" for Senator Bill Leonard, a Republican. I received recognition in Sacramento and was given the opportunity to sit with the Assemblyman and vote.

"What you owe yourself cannot be deposited in the bank"

11. I received the "Leader in Education" award from California State University, San Bernardino. This award was presented to graduates who have given outstanding services in the field of education.

"I will carry the torch for our youth"

12. I can be found in the United States of America, Congressional Record, proceedings and debates of the 103rd Congress, 1st Session of the House of Representatives, where Congressman George Brown gave tribute to me and others for outstanding services to the Inland Empire.

"Show me, lead me, and help me make a difference"

13. I was recognized by The Precious Foundation of Tomorrow for outstanding contributions and services to the youth of the community and the world.

"I'm always tripping over success"

14. Students and staff found it fitting to create a dynasty for students. The dream was to develop a business plan to establish a restaurant. Collaboration with the San Bernardino City Unified School District's Nutrition Services, California State University and San Bernardino Valley College led to the establishment of Maggie's Café, named in my honor. This, of course, led to the establishment of Maggie's Kids Foundation.

"I stand up and sit down for what I believe in"

15. I received the second "Values in Education" award presented by the Learning for Life Foundation of the Inland Empire. This award was presented for outstanding leadership in the field of education. The Learning for Life Foundation is associated with the Boys Scouts of America.

"Remember my deeds. They mean a lot to me"

16. I received an appreciation award from the Male Involvement Program which is sponsored by the San Bernardino Public Health Department. This award was given for making a difference in the lives of young men.

"Smile and say thanks. I've done my best"

17. I was invited to visit with an educational committee in Washington, DC, to talk about school accountability. I was invited by Congressman Joe Baca and met with a senator from Mississippi. This gave the three of us who were invited from this area a chance to speak about education in our districts and listen to the educational concerns presented by representatives from Mississippi.

"Help me learn to help you and me"

18. I have been nominated to represent the Highland's Women's Club as its first African-American president. This organization of women who live in Highland was organized over one hundred years ago.

"It takes time to make a difference"

19. I received the "Soror of the Year" award (twice) from the National Sorority of Phi Delta Kappa, Inc., Delta Rho Chapter. This award is presented to a member who has given over and above what is expected during the sorority year.

"Sisters doing for themselves and others."

20. I received the YMCA President's Award in recognition of Dedicated Services. This award was presented to me for my leadership in keeping the San Bernardino YMCA open so that our youth could continue swimming lessons and

our seniors could continue with their therapeutic swimming.

"Never stop chasing your dreams"

21. I was named one of the "Ten Who Made a Difference." This award was presented by the Sun newspaper in honor of residents of San Bernardino County who had contributed to the success of the community.

"Taking dreams to a new level"

22. I submitted a letter of interest to serve on the San Bernardino City Unified School District's Citizens' Bond Oversight Committee. I was not only selected, but I was voted to be the Chair of this nine-member committee. Our task is to keep the community informed, review expenditures and provide an annual audit on the $140 million dollar bond that was issued to build and renovate schools. It is a good feeling to know that one can be involved in the education of K-12 students by making sure there is a safe environment for learning.

"You can make a difference even outside the box"

23. I had the opportunity to meet former President Bill Clinton during his first term of office. I felt quite special being in his presence while he was a visitor in San Bernardino. I had the opportunity to shake his hands and receive his warm smile.

"Life is what life is. Learn what "is" is"

24. I became a candidate for the third highest position in the National Sorority of Phi Delta Kappa, Inc. I had the opportunity to travel to four of the five regions and made presentations regarding my reasons for wanting to be the

Second Supreme Anti-Basileus (vice president). Even though I was the unknown candidate, I am pleased with the warm reception I received from those throughout the United States.

"Meet the challenges"

25. I am one of a few who is not a native of California to say that I know the first African-American principal and superintendent in the state. Dorothy Inghram is a friend of mine and calls me annually about the Friends of Dorothy Inghram Library Fashion Show/Luncheon. She is 105 years young as of this writing. Her father was the founder of the first African American Episcopal Church in San Bernardino.

"Believe in others who believe in you"

26. Maggie's Café was named in my honor and is currently providing a service to the students at San Andreas High School. These students were getting hands-on training in short order cooking, dishwashing, use of the cash register, etc.

"Do all you can with love and care"

27. I received a call from California State University, San Bernardino, and the University of Redlands, asking me to teach a class on both campuses for the administrative training program. This was quite an honor and since I feel there are a number of administrators who should have chosen another career path. It gave me an opportunity to let the class participants know that if they do not have compassion for students, they need to leave the profession now. Unfortunately, there have been a few of them in the program at both institutions. I'm sure they know who they are.

"Do what you love and love what you do"

28. Project P.R.I.D.E. (Parents Responsibility in Developing Ethics) was created to assist parents determined to make their children successful citizens. The process involves holistic services to all members of the family. This is not the traditional parenting program where a group of strangers come together to talk about their children, but a program where parents get to be a part of the team in a leadership role.

"This is what you do when the shoe doesn't fit"

29. I received the Town and Gown Award from the University of Redlands. This award is presented to citizens who have worked diligently to improve the community. This award was exceptionally special since I was recommended by Dorothy Inghram, the first African-American superintendent in the State of California.

"Make friends while making a difference"

30. I was asked to serve as a commissioner by the Supervisor of the Fifth District of San Bernardino County. The five commissioners met monthly to hear from each agency to make sure that fair and equal hiring/promotion practices are in place.

"If not me, who?"

31. I worked for the San Bernardino City Unified School District for thirty-two years; and while all assignments were challenging and exciting, my last sixteen at San Andreas are the ones I will talk about. The students have many needs and the certificated and classified staff members were more than willing to assist all students. Even though we have students who have gone to prison (two for murder) and several are deceased (a few from illnesses but most from violence), many have continued their education to make this world a better place.

"To care and to share is a blessing"

32. I continue to serve as a member of the YMCA Corporate Board proud to be a charter member of the Highland Family YMCA board. This will give me an opportunity to continue collaborating with the San Bernardino YMCA also. The services provided will improve the quality of life for all of the citizens.

"Approach progress with tender hands"

33. Getting family information from my cousin, Randolph Peete, is rewarding and exciting as I learn about my heritage. He has provided me with names that I have never heard and events that I did not know occurred. It is regrettable that he passed away before I completed this book.

"How great thou art"

34. I was one of many selected to interview for the Board of Trustees for the San Bernardino Community College District. The interviews were opened to the public and a lottery system was used to determine the order of the interview. While I was the first one to be interviewed, I also had the opportunity to hear the other candidates. It was a good feeling to be one of the candidates in the last round before a selection was made. Even though I did not receive the appointment, it gave me a good feeling about being considered until the very end.

"Feel good about feeling bad"

35. Elementary school employees always get gifts from students and parents because that is just the thing to do. Middle school students will give a gift from time to time because you managed to keep the bullies from destroying them. Many of these gifts come with support from parents. High school students, especially seniors, will give you a gift when they know you are the reason they managed to graduate and possibly get a scholarship. I am proud to say that after teaching three years at California State University, San Bernardino, I received a plaque from the Public Relations class, spring of 2005, expressing their thanks to me as a professor. Thanks to all of you.

36. I received the pioneer in education award from the Delta Sigma Theta Sorority.

37. I was part of the team that wrote the policy to provide an education for African American students to close the achievement gap.

38. I was one of 36 Women of Achievement recognized by 36th Assemblyman Bill Emmerson.

39. I was appointed to the Community Hospital of San Bernardino Board and previously served as a member of the board for St. Bernardine's Hospital.

40. I was successful in getting a portable building donated to the Charlie Seymour Golf Academy.

~ Chapter Thirteen ~

Cherries and Cherry Pits

Life for me has not been a bowl of cherries, but when you take out the pits, it has not been bad. I can remember a number of instances where God was more than good to me.

When I was under the age of ten, I can remember when my brother threw a clay pitcher and hit me just below the eye. Had he thrown it a little harder and a little higher, I would have probably lost my eye.

We use to play cowboys and Indians and would jump from the roof of the house. I never received a broken limb.

I also remember the time that I stuck a hair pin in an electrical socket and was going to use another pin to remove it. My mother entered the room just in time.

When I was between the ages of ten and twelve, I remember my siblings were chasing a mule and asked me to stand on the opposite side of the gate and not let the mule pass. Of course I thought I could stop this stubborn animal. At least I was smart enough to jump out of the way.

I went to the beach with my family and my oldest brother took us out in the water where the water covered my head. I got scared and he told me to just go back to shore. I was lucky that a wave did not come and knock me down since I didn't know how to swim.

Between the ages of twenty and thirty, I would horseback ride each Sunday. One Sunday, Ginger did not want me on her back obviously, so she ran out of the trail area, jumped a fence and kept rapid speed as she continued in the forest area. I just held on and kept myself close to her neck saying, "You dumb horse. If you kill me, you will kill yourself first." One of the ranch supervisors saw the run-away horse and rescued me.

Another incident involved my car. I was driving to the Ford Motor Plant when one car appeared to be coming at me while I was on a bridge. My car hit the bridge walk and was just inches from tumbling into the river.

I was going out with friends on a fishing expedition. We had gotten on the chartered boat and had been out to sea about ten minutes when a storm came up and visibility was zero. I was aware that a Navy ship was close by but did not panic until the captain said we were lost. We stayed in the ocean for one hour before we were able to dock and that was about two miles from where we started. We had to be bused to our starting point.

While in New York City, it is always a thrill to ride the subway. This particular day, the subway stopped quickly and the conductor asked everyone to get out. What we discovered was that another train was on the track and had we continued, we would have hit it.

After forty, my life became a little more comfortable and safe. But one day when I was on my way to visit my former secretary and a car pulled in front of me and I could not stop. The impact caused a fire and my airbag deployed. Even though my car was totaled, my body was just bruised from the airbag.

While announcing the parade in honor of Black History month, the music from the bands, drill teams, and drum squads excited two horses, which broke down the fence and began running through the crowd at a rapid speed. I saw the horses approaching the area of the announcement booth, but fortunately, they continued on their way. The scare made it difficult to continue announcing, but we managed.

We have been blessed in many ways. Sometimes we know it, sometimes we don't. In spite of all of my shortcomings, things could have been worse. In regard to my successes, things could have been better. I would like to instill in my readers to take what is offered and use it to benefit those you come in contact with.

The poem below is an original and is dedicated to all of you. Use whatever message you interpret from it to guide your life and make you a better person. It is my desire to get you to see what a wonderful world we live in and our job is to change the negative attitude of the people who live with us.

Lead the way or show me how
I cannot do it alone.
Bad attitudes and poor dispositions
Will only make me moan.

Please don't look the other way.
The concerns still exist.
Opportunities are great, mighty great,
And this you don't want to miss.

God put us all here for a reason,
And we are not to question why.
There are so many things we should reap
Long before we die.

Take heed my brothers and sisters too.
There are obstacles you must face:
Believing in yourself and what you can do
To empower the human race.

~ Chapter Fourteen ~

Now Let's Hear it from Some of the Students

I remember I had the credits to graduate and I did something stupid and Mrs. Hill found out about it...She told me that I had to write an essay or I could not walk at graduation. I stressed over this for two weeks and I finally wrote the paper and gave it to her at graduation along with flowers and an apology. I later found out that right after I gave her the paper, she tossed it in the trash can and went on with the graduation ceremony.

My parents told me this story. I must say I am deeply appreciative of what you tolerated from me and I only hope that you can influence the masses from the top. You are an inspiration of human dignity and respect and everyone who knows you cannot dispute these words of your character and being. You challenged those lost in youth with outstanding results and these people leaving messages today are only a testament to your greatness. Saying thank you is not enough but it is all I can do. So thank you, thank you, and thank you!"

"All things are possible when you try your hardest to learn something every day and be successful"

"I'm one of your old students. You're the best! I remember your wonderful stories. I still have a little book you gave me filled with stories about little life lessons. Thank you for being one of my most memorable teachers who impact me wisely."

"When I first met Mrs. Hill at San Andreas I remember sitting in her office with my Mom and being scared. I didn't think she would let me in because she seemed very strict and serious about whom she let into her school. I think it was because she wanted her students to make it to graduation. By the time many of us got to San Andreas, it was our last hope. I mean honestly we were a bunch of screw ups in school. But, Mrs. Hill gave us that chance to make it to graduation

and she saw something in us that no one else could."

"I remember you, Mrs. Hill! I remember how you always had positive things to say to each student. I live behind an elementary school and think about who will guide these kids the way you did for us."

"I will never forget the day you crushed my ego and introduced me to humility. You see, you allowed me to come to San Andreas and with 65 credits needed to graduate and graduation was June. I was told I would have to go to Summer school and another year, which would cause me to not fulfill my Army reserve contract. You once said "No task is impossible if you want it bad enough. How bad do you want to graduate?" On the 15th of May I came in with my last and final 5 credit slip from one of my teachers and when I came into your office all full of myself, you tore up the slip and said, "I don't think you deserve this." I was drop jawed and dumb founded. You then told me Never Get Full of yourself....But never let any tell you.... YOU CAN'T DO IT!!!!! And with that handed me my graduation slip, while the whole office laughed and congratulated me.

I have over twenty years in the army and looking at possibly retiring soon. This next year, I have been told I would make a great teacher...And I owe my life and knowledge to women and teachers like you. You have instilled in me the fundamentals needed in life to survive and know the difference between right and wrong. I thank you; for you are the reason I can teach young soldiers what they need to protect our great Nation. You cared enough to give us, the young misguided and misunderstood students, an opportunity to reach for the stars.

Thank you for all you have and will do. I pray my children have someone to listen, teach and love as you did for us."

~ Chapter Fifteen ~

One of my Favorite Speeches

I was invited to make a speech to an audience of young men who are fathers. I feel there is a crisis with our young, especially those who are still in high school and those who have dropped out of school. The conference was cancelled so let me share with you what I was going to say. Small revisions have been made for this printing. I hope our young readers get to the end of my book, if not, please let them know about this speech.

~ All Daddies

are Not Men But all Fathers must be Fathers ~

In the beginning, God created heaven and earth and when things were almost perfect, man was created, according to the Bible. A short time later, someone said, "Whoa man, you have a big job ahead of you". So let the following be known:

Time has brought about many changes
Some have been quite grand,
Others have met various disasters
Due to the challenges of man.

Men have and will continue to make a difference
Even though some say, "Why bother".
It's an important ingredient in our society
Because of the love of one's father.

I appreciate you for reading my message

And hope it is well understood.
Being a positive role model in our children's lives
Isn't that a part of Fatherhood?

21 REASONS YOU NEED TO BE A FATHER

1. ON SCHOOL

How can you help close the achievement gap when you don't even know there is a gap? Your job is to assist your child in school. This is the responsibility of the parent as well as the school and the community.

2. ON JOBS

Where can you find a job using one hand since you need the other one to hold up your pants? When your children watch you, they think they can only prepare for the one-handed jobs.

Who will hire someone who can do everything? Where is that on the job announcement? Will your children be willing and ready to work when all they see you do is watch television, play video games, visit your unemployed friends and go visit friends in jail? Do they think you are working so hard, you are too tired to come home from jail or prison at night?

3. ON RETIREMENT

Life expectancy for all males is over the age of sixty. Isn't that a little too old to have a key to your parents' house?

4. ON COLLEGE

Even if your child makes it through high school and get a scholarship to college, how will you know if everything is in place? What do you know about SAT and ACT scores? What do you know about Pell Grants and other financial aid? Will you be able to purchase education insurance?

5. ON HOME OWNERSHIP

Do you think your children do not deserve a back yard? Where is the playground swings, etc.? Children deserve their own bedroom, a quiet place to study, and a quiet place to read.

6. ON MUSIC

When did your child learn The Star Spangled Banner and do you know the words? Was it replaced with whatever is on TV or the radio?

7. ON INSURANCE

Who will take care of the medical bills? Why don't I just ask you now: When did you have your last checkup? When did you visit your dentist? Are there any cavities, need for a root canal, cleaning, etc.? One day you might have to pay for false teeth.

8. ON THE BIRDS AND THE BEES

We all know about the stork but how do you avoid becoming a daddy at a young age?

9. ON THE FIRST DATE

Who can better tell you of the pitfalls of a first date than a parent? Do you want your daughter going out with someone who does not know how to open and hold the door, take off his hat in the restaurant or movie, or not know which fork to use with the salad and which one for the mail meal? Do you want your son to take out a girl who does not know how to sit properly or one who will chew gum during the movie or dinner?

10. <u>ON VOTING</u>

    How old do you really have to be to participate in the democratic process?

11. <u>WALKING THE BRIDE/GROOM DOWN THE AISLE</u>

    Not only should there be a wedding, but someone has to pay for it. How much does a gown cost? What about the pre-wedding dinner? Who rents the tuxedos and who pays for the honeymoon? What about the cost of the music, dinner, flowers, minister, etc.? What about your suit? Will you be in a position to take care of your expenses?

12. <u>BUYING A CAR</u>

    Now this is a good one. I can hear you saying, "Save your money if you want a car. Money doesn't grow on trees, you know."

13. <u>ON PUBERTY</u>

    Now this one is really fun because you can still remember what you were doing at this age and most likely is the reason you have a child today.

14. <u>ON MOVING OUT OF THE HOUSE</u>

    Remember the old say, "Visitors are like fish. After three days, they both stink". Well, we give our children a few more days, months and years but the day will come that you will want them out of the house and believe it or not, they are ready to leave. Are they ready to survive on their own? Don't you think if you prepare them well, you will enjoy your new office (their former bedroom) a lot better?

15. ON TELEVISION

Unless it is educational, turn off the tube and grab a book. You should model by reading with your children daily.

16. ON BULLYING

Life just isn't like it use to be. Bullying use to mean that you got in a fight got a bloody nose or a busted lip and a torn shirt. When you got home and your parents asked what happened,"You said, nothing," Now the bullies are cowards and they carry guns and knives. Teach your children how to deal with bullies so that you want have to pick them up from jail or identify them in the morgue.

17. ON DRINKING

Please do not encourage your children to drink and make sure they do not see you in an intoxicated stage. Just because it is legal doesn't mean it is a good thing to do. Please encourage your children to read the side effects.

18. ON DRUGS

This is not legal and should never be encouraged. Don't use the excuse that it is better than taking a drink. This includes prescription medicine as well. Encourage your children to read the side effects.

19. ON FATHERING A CHILD

When is a good time to consider fatherhood? It is after you get an education, become a permanent and productive employee, and ready to assume the duties of a father for a minimum of eighteen years.

20. <u>ON SERVICE TO YOUR COUNTRY</u>

    There is still a selective service commitment for all males at age 18. Make sure you understand your duties and obligations to your country.

21. <u>ON BEING A PART OF THE VILLAGE</u>

    Yes, I know you've heard it. It does take a village to raise a child. If you are the father, you should be in the front row at all events. Know your family and your neighbors as they also are part of the village.

One of the best fathering tips is to love and/or respect your children's mother and let your children witness this respect. Children remember what they see and what they hear. Don't forget to pass on your skills, especially those that have made or will make you an excellent father. Instill in children virtue habits that are the essentials of good character and morals.

In conclusion, please remember:

- You do not have a right to bring a child in this world unless you can provide adequate housing, sufficient food, and clothing for this person.
- You do not have the right to bring a child in this world unless you are willing to make him/her a better person than you are.
- You do not have a right to bring a child in this world unless you are willing to provide moral, ethics, and value training to him/her.
- You do not have a right to bring a child in this world unless you are fully employed or able to provide legal financial support.
- You do not have a right to bring a child in this world and expect him/her to be a good school citizen when you don't know what being a good citizen is.

- You do not have a right to bring a child in this world if you are not committed to providing quality time.
- You do not have a right to bring a child in this world knowing you are not willing be a part of his/her life.
- You do not have a right to bring a child in this world while you are doing things that will land you in jail.
- You do not have a right to bring a child in this world and neglect him/her by not providing the love and comfort they deserve.
- You do not have a right to even think about bringing a child in this world and expect others to play your role as father.

Fathers come and fathers go

For many reasons they share,

~ But if you aren't ready to be the best father ~

Please leave the bassinet bare.

~ Chapter Sixteen ~

The Best is yet to come!

This is my first attempt at writing a book and while it has taken me more years than I had planned, I felt a need to get something out while I am still of sound mind (I think).

I have much more to tell and hope you will patiently await my next book. It is my intent to gain the motivation after completing my first one. It is important that I inform you of the following:

- My early school days where I attended a two-room segregated school where two teachers gave us the best possible education. I also attended a segregated high school where I had my first male teacher and was able to graduate from high school at the age of sixteen.
- My college days where I participated in sit-in demonstrations where we were not allowed to eat at the lunch counters in major stores. It was during that time we had separate facilities in the bus stations.
- My first job in California and how it influenced my community and political volunteerism.
- My first teaching position, administrative assignments and other official duties that contributed to the success of many students who are very successful citizens.
- The creation of Maggie's Café and Maggie's Kids Foundation.
- Why my first night's session with prospective administrators was more of a sermon than a class

assignment. These are classes that I taught for California State University, San Bernardino, and the University of Redlands.
- The diagnosis of cancer and how I did not let it stop me from being me.
- Why I wrote my eulogy.

We must remember that we must nurture these virtues in ourselves first, and them be role models for our youth who truly depend upon us to give all we are capable of giving. It is our duty and obligation to make this world a better place for all of us to live and prosper.

I appreciate my family members reading this short book in its entirety. I know you have been looking for your name. You were in my thoughts even if you were not in print except in the beginning of the book.

While this writing has been a joy, I have not given it my best. I ask your forgiveness if you feel this book was not worth the $10; however, I am not making enough to give you a refund and donate to Maggie's Kids Foundation and a scholarship fund.

This book has been written at a level that all middle and high school students, no matter their reading level, will be able to comprehend. I hope the spoken words of the students and the writer will motivate all students to stay in school. If we did it, so can you.

The End